A Da Capo Press Reprint Series

**FRANKLIN D. ROOSEVELT
AND THE ERA OF THE NEW DEAL**
GENERAL EDITOR : FRANK FREIDEL
Harvard University

—————

THE
MIGRATORY-CASUAL
WORKER

Division of Research
Work Projects Administration

Research Monographs

Works Progress Administration
Division of Social Research
Research Monograph VII

THE MIGRATORY-CASUAL WORKER

By John N. Webb

DA CAPO PRESS • NEW YORK • 1971

A Da Capo Press Reprint Edition

This Da Capo Press edition of *The Migratory-Casual Worker* is an
unabridged republication of the first edition published in Washington,
D.C., in 1937. It is reprinted by permission from a copy of the original
edition owned by the Harvard College Library.

Library of Congress Catalog Card Number 73-165690
ISBN 0-306-70339-4

Published by Da Capo Press, Inc.
A Subsidiary of Plenum Publishing Corporation
227 West 17th Street, New York, N.Y. 10011
All Rights Reserved

Manufactured in the United States of America

THE
MIGRATORY-CASUAL
WORKER

WORKS PROGRESS ADMINISTRATION
DIVISION OF SOCIAL RESEARCH

THE MIGRATORY-CASUAL WORKER

By

JOHN N. WEBB
Coordinator of Urban Research

Research Monograph VII

UNITED STATES
GOVERNMENT PRINTING OFFICE
WASHINGTON : 1937

Works Progress Administration

HARRY L. HOPKINS, *Administrator*

CORRINGTON GILL, *Assistant Administrator*
HOWARD B. MYERS, *Director*
Division of Social Research

LETTER OF TRANSMITTAL

WORKS PROGRESS ADMINISTRATION,
Washington, D. C., April 2, 1937.

SIR: I have the honor to transmit a report on the economic and personal characteristics of migratory-casual workers in agriculture and industry. The information presented is derived from a study conducted by the Federal Emergency Relief Administration during the operation of the Transient Relief Program. This report is one of a series of investigations being conducted by agencies of the Government to assist in fulfilling the provisions of Senate Resolution 298, 74th Congress, 2d Session, which directs the Secretary of Labor "to study, survey, and investigate the social and economic needs of laborers migrating across State lines."

This study was made by the Division of Social Research, under the direction of Howard B. Myers, Director of the Division. The collection and tabulation of the data were supervised by John N. Webb, Coordinator of Urban Research, with the assistance of Katherine Gordon and Howard R. Ogburn.

The report was prepared by John N. Webb and edited by Malcolm J. Brown and Orin C. Cassmore. Special acknowledgment is made of the assistance rendered by Greta E. Mueller and Awilda Shorter in the preparation of the field schedule and in the development of the interviewing procedures. Acknowledgment is also made to the supervisors in the several cities in which this survey was made, and to many others who cooperated in the work of preparing this report.

Respectfully submitted.

CORRINGTON GILL,
Assistant Administrator.

HON. HARRY L. HOPKINS,
Works Progress Administrator.

CONTENTS

TEXT TABLES

Contents

SUPPLEMENTARY TABLES
(Appendix)

INTRODUCTION

THIS REPORT on the migratory-casual worker is a byproduct of the studies of the transient unemployed conducted by the research section of the Division of Research, Statistics, and Finance, Federal Emergency Relief Administration, during 1934 and 1935.[1] In the process of determining the characteristics of unattached individuals and family groups receiving aid from the Transient Relief Program, it was found that a fairly clear line could be drawn between those for whom migration was an expedient of a few months, and those for whom migration was a customary way of obtaining a living. The distinction—which was fully established in the report on the transient unemployed—was between a group of depression transients composed of temporary migrants, and a permanent supply of mobile workmen made up of habitual migrants.

Because the depression transient represented by far the more important problem from the point of view of relief administration, a report on his characteristics became the first objective of the study conducted by the research section. When this task was completed, however, there was time for, and interest in, a supplementary report on the unattached migratory-casual worker. Although much more limited in scope than the preceding report, it is believed that this account of the migratory-casual worker will contribute to the increasing body of knowledge about the more mobile portion of our working population.

When the Transient Relief Program was initiated in 1933, the composition of the mobile "army of unemployed" was unknown. The grave national emergency existing at that time did not permit delay until the nature and needs of the nonresident unemployed could be studied. It was common knowledge that migratory-casual workers were poorly paid and underemployed during the best of times; and it was natural to expect that they comprised a substantial portion of the needy nonresidents in 1933. But in initiating a relief program for nonresidents the Federal Emergency Relief Administration felt that there were valid reasons for making a distinction between "bona fide transients" and "seasonal migratory workers." It was

---

[1] See Webb, John N., The Transient Unemployed, Research Monograph III, Division of Social Research, Works Progress Administration, Washington, D. C., 1936. A second report, dealing more extensively with migrant family groups, is in process of preparation.

believed that failure to make this distinction would provide a subsidy to those industries that existed and benefited in some degree
because of the cheap labor supply furnished by migratory-casual
workers. In September 1933, the Federal Emergency Relief Administration sent to the State Emergency Relief Administrations a memorandum (No. A–1) which stated, in part:

> Federal funds now available to the several States for the care of
> transients require that the utmost vigilance be employed in assuring
> that these funds be applied to the treatment of bona fide transients.
> A number of States have, in the past, encouraged the employment of
> seasonal migratory workers in various industrialized types of agricul-
> ture * * *. The funds available for transients are * * * not
> intended for this type of nonresident.

As it turned out, this distinction was unnecessary in the first place,
and impossible of strict enforcement in the second place. As soon
as the Transient Relief Program had been in operation long enough
to permit some study of the migrant population it was discovered
that the depression transient,[2] rather than the migratory-casual
worker, made up the great bulk of applicants for nonresident relief.
But even if this had not been the case it is difficult to see how the
distinction between the "migratory worker" and the "transient"
would have been enforced in practice. Certainly there was little in
outward appearance, mode of travel, and nature of needs to distinguish one type of migrant from the other. In fact, unless the
migratory-casual worker voluntarily identified himself as such, there
was no way, at the time he applied for relief, by which transient
bureau officials could be certain that they were following the provisions of memorandum A–1. At least one-half of all unattached
transients given relief remained under care less than 1 week, and a
considerable proportion, only 1 night. Careful investigation of an
applicant's claims for relief was impossible unless he remained at the
bureau for 1 week or more, and in practice, an investigation was not
attempted for the more mobile (short-stay) transients. Therefore,
the migratory-casual worker had little difficulty in obtaining aid from
the transient program when there was no other alternative.

The surprising—and instructive—fact is that only a small proportion of the habitual migratory-casual labor supply made use of
this alternative. The migratory-casual worker is on the margin
of subsistence most of the time and, when in need, is even more
clearly a nonresident in the local poor law sense of the term than was
the depression transient. Nevertheless, the real migratory-casual

---

[2] Those eligible for assistance under the transient program were defined as "all persons
in need of relief who have not resided within the boundaries of a State for 12 consecutive
months."

worker made up only a small fraction of the total transient relief population.[3]

The explanation of this fact is partly economic and partly personal. A substantial portion of the occupations followed by the migratory-casual worker continued to provide some employment throughout the depression. The experienced migrant knew where and when he was most likely to find a job in the grain and fruit harvests, logging operations, shipping, road construction and maintenance, and other seasonal activities; and he continued to migrate to those places even though he knew the pay would be less than in previous years. This knowledge, plus a strong personal antipathy to being found in "soup lines", helps to explain why the confirmed migratory-casual worker kept out of transient bureaus except for occasional overnight stops or an unusually bad run of luck in finding employment.

The fact that the confirmed migratory-casual worker did obtain assistance from the Transient Relief Program makes this report possible. The 13 cities[4] which served as the sources of information for the study of the transient unemployed included the country's most important centers for migratory-casual workers. During the first half of 1935, careful records were made of the work histories and itineraries of migratory-casual workers registered for relief in the transient bureaus of these 13 cities. Some of the records taken were unsuited for study because the worker either could not, or would not, give a complete account of his employment and itinerary during 1933 and 1934. Other records were excluded because the worker supplying the information was on the margin between the temporary and the habitual migrant. Still a third type of record could not be used because the worker had obviously either deliberately misstated his history—a not uncommon occurrence in the experience of the Transient Relief Program—or had drawn too freely upon his imagination.

After a careful weeding-out process there were available 500 records suitable for study. All of the 13 cities in the transient relief survey were represented, but nearly three-fifths of the histories came from 4 of the cities—Seattle, Denver, Memphis, and Minneapolis. The number and type of workers interviewed in each of the 13 cities may be found in appendix table 1.

The 500 individuals whose records are used in this report do not represent a sample of migratory-casual workers in a strict statistical sense. Indeed, it is difficult to see how such a sample could be

---

[3] See The Transient Unemployed, op. cit., pp. 66–67.

[4] Boston, Chicago, Dallas, Denver, Jacksonville (Fla.), Kansas City (Mo.), Los Angeles, Memphis, Minneapolis, New Orleans, Phoenix, Pittsburgh, and Seattle.

obtained. The total number of migratory-casual workers is unknown; the membership of this mobile labor supply changes from
month to month; and the individuals that make up this group are
on the move so much of the time that they provide none of the
opportunities common among stable populations for selecting a
demonstrably representative group. Only when the migratory-
casual worker comes within the range of some fact-finding agency,
such as existed during the survey of the transient unemployed, can
his characteristics be observed without a great deal of difficulty.

No purpose would be served by assuming that the 500 individuals
contributing factual evidence for this report were completely representative of the hundreds of thousands of migratory-casual workers
who, each year, are employed in seasonal activities. But at the same
time there is no good reason for believing that the characteristics
of these 500 workers were so peculiar that an account of their work
histories and itineraries would lead to markedly erroneous conclusions. It is true that these workers were receiving relief at the
time the records were taken. But their employment histories provide convincing evidence that their relief was largely incidental. It
is also true that the several cities in which records were taken are
unequally represented in the study, and this circumstance has a
definite effect on the work patterns discussed in chapter II. But
the fact that more satisfactory records could be obtained in, say,
Seattle than in Boston can hardly be considered a disqualifying
bias since Seattle is a well-known concentration point for migratory-
casual workers and Boston is not.

The point of this discussion is simply to issue a warning against
accepting the conclusions of the study uncritically. Those respon-
sible for this report are keenly aware of the limitations imposed by
the small number of cases and the methods by which these cases
were selected. As far as the records are concerned, they are unusually good. The field work was done by a staff of interviewers
that had a wide experience with, and a real understanding of, the
man on the road. Therefore, it can be said with confidence that
the 500 records are accurate; and, as the second part of this report
will show, these records present information not available from
other sources.

The plan of this report needs some comment. Chapter I presents
a general and nonstatistical description of the migratory-casual
worker and his place in the labor supply. The remaining chapters
are devoted to a statistical description of the 500 workers whose
histories were selected for study. Specifically, the statistical section
of this report is arranged as follows: The extent of migration and
the work patterns of the 500 workers are presented and discussed in

chapter II; the next chapter is devoted to a discussion of such characteristics as amount, duration, and seasonality of migratory-casual employment, and net yearly earnings; chapter IV carries this description farther by presenting detailed information on specific types of work done; chapter V deals with some of the personal characteristics of the 500 workers; and the final chapter presents the major conclusions of the study. For those readers who would like to obtain a brief statement of the content of this report, a short summary of the principal findings follows.

SUMMARY

THIS STUDY of the migratory-casual worker grew out of a survey of the transient unemployed made during the operation of the Transient Relief Program of the Federal Emergency Relief Administration. In the process of determining the characteristics of individuals receiving aid from the Transient Relief Program, it was found that a clear distinction could be made between those for whom migration was an expedient of a few months and those for whom migration was an established way of obtaining a living.

The distinction was not based upon outward appearance, for in this respect there was little to distinguish one type of migrant—depression transient, tramp, or migratory-casual worker—from the other. Instead, the distinction was made principally on the basis of two characteristics: (1) the type of work done and (2) the work habit or pattern. Considered jointly, these two characteristics made it possible to distinguish the migratory-casual worker from the mobile nonworker, or tramp; and from the temporarily mobile job-seeker, or transient unemployed of the depression period.

The true migratory-casual worker travels regularly over a relatively large area and is dependent for a living on work that is distinctly seasonal or intermittent, and, for the most part, casual in nature. In brief, it is the combination of habitual migration with short-time employment that distinguishes the migratory-casual worker from all other types of workers in the labor supply. Wherever the local labor supply is inadequate or unwilling to harvest the grain, the fruit, and the vegetable crops, build and repair the highways and the railroads, repair the levees and build the dams for flood control, fell the logs for lumber, and work the mines and quarries—in all these pursuits and in others the migratory-casual worker provides a supply of cheap and mobile labor upon which these industries are dependent in part, but for which they accept little or no responsibility.

This study shows that the habitual migratory-casual worker is the result of a complex of factors. Both economic and personal motivations are involved, and the two are closely interrelated. On the economic side, the migratory-casual worker is the result of (1) the progression of the seasons, which provides an irregular sequence of employment over a large area, and (2) the pool of unemployment, which rises and falls with business conditions, but which is never completely drained. This combination of circumstances creates the mobility that breaks the stabilizing ties of industrial and community attachment, and at the same time creates a chaotic labor market characterized by substandard wages and working conditions.

On the personal side, the migratory-casual worker is the result of factors that are known but are difficult of precise statement because of their intangibility and because of the wide variety of worker-types represented. Among migratory-casual workers is to be found the militant worker who believes that his position in the labor supply is the result of a failure of the economic system—and particularly of employers—to accept responsibility for the way in which the productive process operates. There is also the apathetic worker to whom the gradual transition from regular employment in industry to a haphazard search for such employment, and finally to a regular pattern of migration, has brought a lessening of ambition and a lack of interest in the future. Perhaps it can only be said that, in general, it is essential to the migratory-casual worker that he move, that no one environment claim him long, that scenes be new and persons different. These desires, expressed or only vaguely felt, are the core of his existence and the governor of his activity.

Analysis of 500 work histories for the years 1933 and 1934 has provided information on several important aspects of the mobility and employment characteristics of the migratory-casual worker. The more important items of information may be summarized as follows: Interstate migration was the rule among the 500 workers; in each of the 2 years—1933 and 1934—about two-thirds of them crossed at least 1 State line, and one-fourth crossed at least 6 State lines.

Migratory-casual workers following agricultural employment exclusively were less mobile than were workers employed principally at industrial pursuits or those combining in about equal proportions agricultural and industrial employment.

The number of State-line crossings reported by the 500 workers in each year was in sharp contrast to the number of States in which they actually obtained employment. Somewhat over one-half of the 500 workers found jobs in only 1 State and an additional one-fourth found employment in only 2 States; whereas, about one-half of the workers had crossed 1 to 10 State lines and 11 to 15 percent had crossed 11 to 25 State lines.

Maps of the itineraries of these workers show that compactness and regularity of work patterns were distinctly more pronounced among agricultural than among industrial workers. This appears to be the result of the regular and predictable recurrence of agricultural work opportunities in the same area.

The average duration of jobs was about 2 months (including holidays and time lost during employment) in both 1933 and 1934. More jobs lasted 1 to 2 months than any other time interval; about one-half of all jobs lasted from 1 to 3 months; jobs in agriculture were shortest and jobs in industry longest in duration.

The average duration of jobs becomes more significant when considered in view of the number of jobs held. Well over three-fourths of the 500 workers held only 1, 2, or 3 jobs in each of the years 1933 and 1934, and less than one-fifth held more than 3 jobs.

Although there is some demand for migratory-casual workers in each month of the year, the demand is highly seasonal. At the low point in the seasonal decline of activity, reached early in the winter, the 500 workers reported less than 600 man-weeks of employment per month; but at the top of the summertime peak, reached in July, activity had more than doubled, and these workers reported approximately 1,200 man-weeks of employment per month. Despite this increase in activity, however, during the busiest month of either year, only one-half of the potential labor power of the 500 workers was utilized.

It is a common practice among migratory-casual workers to spend part of each year on the road, working or seeking work, and then to withdraw from the labor market during the period, usually in the winter months, when the chances of finding work are small. This practice was followed by a majority of the 500 workers in the study. The median length of the migratory period was 41 weeks. Workers in agriculture had the longest off-season period—averaging 13 weeks; and the combination workers, the shortest—averaging 7 weeks in 1933, and only 4 weeks in 1934.

Necessarily, the migratory-casual worker wastes much time and motion during his migratory period both because of a scarcity of jobs and also because of the lack of proper direction to such jobs as are available. Among the 500 workers, the portion of the migratory period spent in employment averaged 24 weeks in 1933 and 21 weeks in 1934.

In exchange for his labor the migratory-casual worker obtains a meager income at best. When the earnings of the 500 workers were reduced to net yearly income to exclude the uncertain value of perquisites, it was found that although the range was from maintenance to $1,350 a year the most frequent earning was between maintenance and $250 yearly. The agricultural worker had the lowest yearly net earning, averaging $110 in 1933 and $124 in 1934. Industrial workers averaged $257 in 1933 and $272 in 1934. Workers combining agricultural and industrial employment earned on the average $223 net in 1933 and $203 in 1934.

An indication of the relative importance of various crops and processes in providing employment for migratory-casual workers was obtained from employment histories of the 500 workers. The cotton crop was the largest single source of employment among agricultural workers. Next in importance to cotton was fruit; and sugar beets, grain, general farm work, vegetables, and berries followed in the order named. Among industrial workers, logging, gas and oil, and railroad maintenance were the most important sources of industrial employment. Migratory-casual workers dividing their employment almost equally between agriculture and industry found the major part of their employment in general agriculture, road construction, logging, shipping, and grain, in the order of their importance.

The difficulty of reducing the amount of working time lost by migratory-casual workers during migration by dovetailing jobs in various short-time operations can be seen from the fact that the seasonal peaks of activity in these pursuits tend to occur together. Many, in fact, reach their peak within the same month, and the peak activity of the majority occurred between the months of May and September.

The 500 workers were veterans of the road; nearly one-half of them had spent 10 years or more in migratory-casual work, and nearly one-fifth, 20 years or more. Most of these workers were between the ages of 20 and 45 years. Somewhat over three-quarters of them were native white; slightly less than one-tenth were Mexicans; and the balance was made up of foreign white—8 percent, Negroes—5 percent, and others—1 percent.

These statistical descriptions of personal characteristics are supplemented by a series of personal history abstracts and autobiographical accounts of some of the 500 workers. The cases presented in this manner were chosen to represent distinct traits found among migratory-casual workers. The more striking of these are examples of the peculiar urge called wanderlust, the physical and occupational deterioration, a strong antipathy to relief, and the puzzled concern of the workers over the forces to which their economic misfortunes may be attributed.

The evidence of this report points clearly to the conclusion that the migratory-casual worker, despite his independent attitude and his pride in his ability to "get by" on the road, is in fact an underemployed and poorly paid worker who easily and frequently becomes a charge on society. Directly or indirectly, State and local governments are forced to accept some responsibility for individuals in this group. Hospitalization, emergency relief, border patrols, and the policing of jungles and scenes of labor disputes are examples of costs that are borne directly by the public. There is another cost which cannot be assessed in dollars: the existence of a group whose low earnings necessitate a standard of living far below the level of decency and comfort. The presence of such a group in any community, even though for a short time each year, cannot fail to affect adversely the wage level of resident workers who are engaged in the same or similar pursuits.

The solutions most commonly suggested for the problem represented by the migratory-casual worker are (1) assisting the worker to establish employment sequences through directed migrations to employments differing as to time of peak operations and (2) stabilizing the migrant worker through provision of off-season employment in the communities where his principal migratory-casual employment is obtained. The shortcomings of these proposals are that they overlook the fact that the problem of the migratory-casual worker is one aspect of the general problem of unemployment and economic insecurity. The direction of workers to jobs, although it may be of assistance in eliminating some of the needless travel entailed in migratory-casual work, cannot provide jobs when they do not exist. As for the second of the proposals mentioned, it is impossible in most cases to find off-season operations to complement the principal seasonal employment of migratory-casual workers; and although conceivably it would be possible to devise employment to occupy the workers during the off-season, the experience of the past has been that this procedure has led to even more than ordinary exploitation.

It is a conclusion of this study that the most promising means of reducing the intensity of the problem is employment office direction of migratory-casual workers, supplemented, during periods of depressions, by public works projects to absorb the surplus. It also seems likely that unemployment insurance will benefit the migratory-casual worker indirectly by reducing the pressure of resident workmen on the labor market served by the migrant. Aside from these means, there does not appear to be any possibility of full or partial solution short of those eventual and unhurried changes in population patterns that promise to eliminate the economic function of the migratory-casual worker.

CHAPTER I

THE MIGRATORY-CASUAL WORKER
A GENERAL DESCRIPTION

THE MIGRATORY-CASUAL workman is a familiar figure in this country. He is seen along the highways and railroads, in the camp cars of construction gangs, in the tar-papered shacks on the sites of dam and levee projects, in open camps along streams and irrigation ditches. At work, the mobile workman is frequently indistinguishable from the resident workman; en route, he is frequently confused with the confirmed tramp.

During the depression years this confusion was increased by the presence of another migrant group—the transient unemployed. In appearance there was little to distinguish one type of migrant from the other; they rode the freight trains together, hitch-hiked along the highways, and kept to themselves except when according to their standards or needs they applied for work, relief, or "help to get a cup of coffee." Because in most cases tramps, transients, and migratory-casual workers were indistinguishable, the public attitude was one of hostility toward all migrants. The burden of caring for the resident unemployed left communities with little patience and no funds for the needy nonresident, to whom, worker and nonworker alike, the epithet "bum" was freely applied.

The attitude of hostility toward unattached migrants during the depression was natural; but it was based upon a confusion of migrant types that must be viewed separately in order to be understood correctly. The transient was distinctly a depression aspect of widespread unemployment; the tramp is an ever-present result of personal maladjustment to social and economic processes; and the migratory-casual worker is a necessary adjunct to those highly seasonal or intermittent industries that cannot, or will not, support a resident labor force.

It is the unattached migratory-casual worker that is the subject of this report: the mobile worker as distinct from the mobile nonworker, or tramp; the habitual migratory worker at casual, or short-time, jobs in seasonal industries as distinct from the temporarily mobile jobseeker, or transient unemployed, of the depression years. The distinction in a particular case may be difficult to make; frequently the depression transient was in the process of becoming an habitual migratory-casual worker; the migratory-casual worker may become a tramp when he can no longer compete for employment with younger men; and the tramp occasionally works side by side with

1

the migratory-casual when wages are attractive or needs are press-ing. But these distinctions, for all their vagueness in the particular case, are known and applied after a fashion by employers, and occasionally by public officials.

For purposes of description and discussion, the migratory-casual worker needs to be defined as clearly as possible to avoid the con-fusion arising out of the indiscriminate use of the terms "tramp", "hobo", "migratory", and "transient" to describe the man on the road. Care should be taken to avoid the subjectivity which ordinarily creeps into the use of these terms. There is a popular habit of calling persons "workers" when they are needed to harvest a ripened crop, and of referring to them as "bums" during the slack season that follows.[1] A kindred confusion, befogging much of the think-ing of persons who have studied the migratory worker more care-fully, arises out of an attempt to distinguish between the various mobile workers on the basis of a difference in moral fiber. The essence of the moralistic distinction is that the "good" migrants work because of their preference, but that the "lower group" works in spite of its preference. For example:

> The distinction between the two types is * * * one seeks employ-ment and pursues chances to work, the other travels and works as little as possible.[2]

Despite appearances, this sort of definition is largely or altogether subjective, and makes for more confusion than clarity.

Objectively, the migratory-casual worker can be identified by two characteristics: (1) the type of work he does and (2) his work habit or pattern. Neither characteristic is, in itself, sufficient identi-fication. The term "casual employment"[3] is generally used to describe unskilled jobs for which the principal qualifications are bodily vigor and the presence of the worker at the time of hiring.

---

[1] See, for example, the Los Angeles Times' comment, Mar. 13, 1936, on the action of the city of Los Angeles in sending municipal police to the State line to turn back needy persons. The Times, in commending the action, says: "If a labor shortage should de-velop later on, it would be easy to modify the regulations so that *seasonal workers* might be admitted * * *." Meanwhile, the Times favors "ridding the State of *indigent tran-sients.*" [Italics supplied.] On this same theme the San Diego Sun, Mar. 23, 1936, comments sardonically: "The only time a bum is expected to come to California is when we need him as a harvest hand. What right has he to come between seasons?"

[2] Lescohier, Don D., The Labor Market, The Macmillan Co., New York, 1919, p. 270.

See also Shields, Louise F., Problem of the Automobile "Floater", Monthly Labor Review, vol. XXI, no. 4, October 1925, p. 14, who distinguishes "between the migratory workers, who are an economic necessity for harvesting our crops and who deserve the respect and gratitude of the communities they serve, and the automobile tramps who work only long enough to keep from starving and that still lower group—the professional wan-dering beggars." Persons who know the migratory-casual well feel that there is no such sharp distinction between the categories of those who are "an economic necessity" and those who "work only long enough to keep from starving."

[3] "The phrase [casual employment] implies, no doubt, primarily shortness of engage-ment, and, secondarily, engagement of first comers." Beveridge, Sir W. II., Unemploy-ment, Longmans, Green & Co., New York, 1930, p. 98.

The best examples of casual, as distinguished from migratory-casual, workers are found in large industrial and transportation centers: longshoremen on the docks, freight handlers in the railroad yards and warehouses, truck and transfer helpers, common labor on building and street construction, women day workers, and odd-job men. Although there is constant shifting from employer to employer when work is to be had, the movement is confined to one city, or even more frequently to a particular section of one city. Such workers may conveniently be thought of as resident-casuals.

In contrast, the migratory-casual moves from place to place over a relatively large area in search of work that is distinctly casual in nature. In this case it is the habitual migratory-work pattern, taken in conjunction with the casual nature of the employment, that is the distinguishing characteristic of the worker. A migratory-work pattern in itself is not enough; for skilled construction workers, salesmen, accountants, actors, and many others are frequently or persistently migratory in their work habits without becoming part of the migratory-casual labor supply. In brief, it is the combination of habitual migration with casual employment that distinguishes the migratory-casual worker from all other types of workers in the labor supply.

Despite the difficulty of precise definition, the migratory-casual worker exists as an objective fact that can be observed wherever the local labor supply is inadequate or unwilling to harvest the grain, the fruit, and the vegetables, to build and repair the highways and railroads, to repair the levees and build the dams for flood control, to fell the logs for lumber, to work the mines and quarries, and generally to provide the pool of cheap and mobile labor upon which many basic industries are dependent in part, but for which these industries accept little or no responsibility.

Perhaps the best definition of a migratory-casual worker is to be found in a worker's own account of his migration and employment. The migratory-casual worker in agriculture, the largest employer of mobile labor, is clearly defined in the following work history:

July–October 1932. Picked figs at Fresno, Calif., and vicinity. Wages, 10 cents a box, average 50-pound box. Picked about 15 boxes a day to earn $1.50; about $40 a month.

October–December 1932. Cut Malaga and muscat (table and wine) grapes near Fresno. Wages, 25 cents an hour. Average 6-hour day, earning $1.50; about $40 a month.

December 1932. Left for Imperial Valley, Calif.

February 1933. Picked peas, Imperial Valley. Wages, 1 cent a pound. Average 125 pounds a day. Earned $30 for season. Also worked as wagon-man in lettuce field on contract. Contract price, 5 cents a crate repack out of packing house; not field pack. This work paid 60 cents to $1 a day. On account of weather, was fortunate to break even at finish of season. Was paying 50 cents a day room and board.

March–April 1933. Left for Chicago. Stayed a couple of weeks. Returned to California 2 months later.

May 1933. Odd-jobs on lawns, radios, and victrolas at Fresno. Also worked as porter and handy man.

June 1933. Returned to picking figs near Fresno. Wages, 10 cents a box. Averaged $1.50 a day, and earned $50 in 2 months.

August 1933. Cut Thompson's seedless grapes near Fresno for 7 days at 1¼ cents a tray. Earned $11. Picked cotton 1 day, 115 pounds; earned $1.

September–November 1933. Cut Malaga and muscat grapes near Fresno. Wages, 25 cents an hour. Made $30 for season.

December 1933. Picked oranges and lemons in Tulare County, Calif. (Earnings not reported.)

January 1934. Picked oranges at 5 cents per box for small jobs and 25 cents per box for large jobs, Redlands, Calif. Earned $30. Picked lemons at 25 cents an hour.

January 1934. Went to Brawley, Calif. Picked peas at 1 cent a pound. Picked 125–150 pounds a day for 15-day season.

February 1934. Picked grapefruit at 25 cents an hour, Koehler, Calif. Worked 8 hours a day on three jobs for a total of 22 days. Also hauled fertilizer at 25 cents an hour.

March 1934. Worked as helper on fertilizer truck at $2 a day for 20 days, Brawley, Calif.

June 1934. Worked as circus hand with Al G. Barnes Circus for 4 weeks at $4.60 a week and board, Seattle to Wallace, Idaho.

July 1934. Tree shaker at 25 cents an hour, averaged $2 a day for 25 days, near Fresno.

August–October 1934. Picked oranges and lemons at 25 cents an hour, working an average of 6 hours a day, for 60 days, near Fresno.

December 1934. Houseman in hotel, Fresno. Received 50 cents a day and board for 1 month, and 25 cents a day and board for 2 months.

The migratory-casual worker following industrial, as distinct from agricultural, employment is equally well defined by the work history presented below:

June–August 1932. Jackhammer operator, railroad construction, Liberty, Mo. Wages $4.80 a day.

September 1932. Extra gang laborer, railroad, Hays, Kans. Wages $3.20 a day.

October 1932. Extra gang laborer, railroad, Cheyenne, Wyo. Wages $4.50 a day.

February–March 1933. Laborer, pipe-line construction, Topeka, Kans. Wages $3 a day.

April–October 1933. Watchman, building construction, Kansas City, Mo. Wages $1.25 a day.

February–May 1934. Extra gang laborer, railroad, Wamsutter, Wyo. Wages $2 a day.

June–September 1934. Extra gang laborer, railroad, Topeka, Kans. Wages $2.80 a day.

The elements essential to an adequate definition of the migratory-casual worker are explicit or implicit in these two work histories. There is high mobility, in the case of the agricultural worker, amounting to at least 6,000 miles of travel in a single year. There is a preponderance of seasonal jobs requiring little or no skill—jobs that last at best only a few months, but form a recurring work pattern. Earnings are small, even under the most favorable circumstances the total yearly income of these workers amounts to no more than is needed for subsistence. And there is implied in these records another characteristic of the migratory-casual worker which, for want of a better word, must be designated as wanderlust.[4]

Still another characteristic of the migratory-casual worker is illustrated by these work histories. The jobs were confined to a small number of crops and processes. The agricultural worker was primarily a fruit and vegetable worker, despite occasional odd jobs at other pursuits; and the industrial worker was employed exclusively on construction and railroad maintenance jobs. Although in general the migratory-casual worker follows a wider range of employments than those reported above, still there is a distinct concentration of principal activities within a comparatively few productive processes. It may be instructive to identify the most important of these processes.

The Wheat Harvest.

From central Texas to the Canadian border and west to the Pacific coast, wheat was once the most important crop requiring a marked addition to the local labor supply during the harvest season. The widespread use of harvesting machinery in recent years has greatly reduced but has not eliminated the use of migratory-casual workers in the wheat harvest, which, at one time, employed 250,000 of these workers.

Fruit Picking and Packing.

The fruit harvest—apples in Washington and Oregon, citrus fruits in the Southwest and to a lesser extent in Florida, soft fruits (prunes, peaches, etc.) along the Pacific coast, and berries in the Mississippi Valley and on Puget Sound—requires large numbers of migratory-casual workers for short periods of time. Speed, long hours, and some skill are necessary to prevent the loss of these perishable products.[5]

Vegetables.

Large-scale production of lettuce, peas, beans, melons, spinach, onions, and similar truck crops in the Southwest, in Washington, and

---

[4] The migratory-casual worker would describe this characteristic inelegantly, but much more aptly, as an "itching foot."

[5] For an interesting account of the "fruit tramp" see "The Endless Trek" in Migratory Labor in California, State Relief Administration, Division of Special Surveys and Studies, San Francisco. 1936, p. 173 ff.

along the eastern seaboard requires migratory-casual workers for cultivating, harvesting, and packing operations.

Sugar Beets.

In the large sugar-beet areas (e. g., Colorado, California, Montana, Michigan) the greater part of the planting, cultivating, and harvesting operations are performed by migratory-casual workers.[6]

Cotton.

In the Southwest—Texas, Oklahoma, Arizona, and California—migratory-casual workers make up an important part of the labor supply necessary in the harvesting of this basic crop. The extension of large-scale cotton cultivation into these areas is, compared with the Eastern Cotton Belt, a relatively recent development. The large land holdings and the undersupply of seasonal labor in the Southwest are in sharp contrast to the innumerable small farms and the oversupply of low-cost labor that exists upon these small holdings between cotton seasons in the Old South. Until a mechanical cotton-picker is perfected, cotton cultivation in the Southwest seems likely to remain dependent upon a mobile supply of cheap labor.

Railroad Right-of-Way Maintenance and Construction.

Railroad construction, next to agriculture, is one of the best examples of the need for a mobile labor supply. The construction of railroads through sparsely settled or unpopulated areas was possible only by the employment of men who were willing to live and work in isolated places. The transcontinental railroads were built by migratory-casual workers, and, except in the Old South, the extra gangs of the maintenance-of-way departments continue to depend upon migratory-casual workers to a large extent.

Construction of Levees, Roads, Tunnels, and Power and Pipe Lines.

Projects of this type, like the railroad construction of former years, must have a mobile labor supply willing to live on the job and to move with it. Frequently seasonal, and almost always intermittent, construction of this kind cannot depend upon local labor.

Oil and Gas.

Because the peculiar nature of oil and gas deposits operate as an incentive to immediate exploitation, almost every new strike becomes

---

[6] Although this report is concerned only with the unattached migratory-casual worker, it should be noted that the migratory family groups are an important element in the migratory-casual labor supply of agriculture. Sugar-beet production is a case in point.

a boom demanding large numbers of workers in areas frequently remote from population centers. Once the activity of opening a field is over, these emergency workers are free to seek work in another of the fields from Texas to Montana. It is only natural, then, that many oil and gas field workers should be migratory-casuals.

Additional employment for migratory-casual workers in the oil fields is provided by the construction of oil pipe lines, and by maintenance work upon them. The approximately 94,000 miles of oil pipe line,[7] stretching largely through sparsely settled areas, require the services of an extensive body of workers who are willing to keep constantly on the move.

Logging.

Logging is a traditional pursuit of the migratory-casual worker. Like much of the work on railroads, levees, and dams, it depends upon workers who are willing to live together in isolated places without the conveniences of life which resident workmen enjoy. The decline in logging operations in recent years and the employers' policy of bettering the conditions of their camps in order to reduce labor turnover have combined to reduce considerably the number of migratory-casual workers employed.[8]

This list of agricultural and industrial operations dependent to an important extent upon migratory-casual workers is by no means complete. Nevertheless, this list shows that operations requiring a mobile labor supply have in common one or more of the following characteristics:

1. A large demand for unskilled or semiskilled labor.
2. Marked seasonality or irregularity of operations.
3. Location remote from population centers.

1. Most of the work done by migratory-casual workers is of an unskilled or semiskilled nature; and the principal requirements for employment are presence at, or just before, the time of peak operations, and the stamina needed for long hours of manual labor under all kinds of weather and working conditions. Skill in the form of manual dexterity rather than that resulting from apprenticeship and training is required for some types of employment (e. g., fruit packing) but, on the whole, migratory-casual jobs consist of unskilled manual work. This fact is reflected in the low earnings of the group

---

[7] See The Statistical Abstract of the United States, 1935, p. 709.

[8] This policy of bettering conditions, originally the result of aggressive labor organization in the industry, has proved to be profitable enough in terms of reduced labor turnover to persist after the decline in the strength of organized labor in this industry. The policy of making camp life attractive enough in some instances to induce workers to bring their families has also been profitable both through the operation of company-owned houses and stores and through the stabilizing effect on the worker of family and community life.

and in the ease with which recruits are drawn from among the unskilled and inexperienced workers in the resident population.[9]

2. A second basic characteristic shared by these processes is pronounced seasonality or irregularity of operation. Employment in agriculture is characterized by seasonality, rather than irregularity, of labor demand and each year a variety of crops requires a large labor force for short periods of intense activity. Formerly, sharp seasonal peaks in employment were caused by the harvesting, and to some extent by the planting, of staples. Although in recent years mechanization (e. g., use of the combine, tractor, etc.) has reduced the fluctuations in the labor demand of staples, a widespread and persistent demand for short-time agricultural labor has arisen as a result of the increase in intensive cultivation of specialty crops. When such crops as vegetables, fruits, and berries are grown on a large scale, and particularly when they must be harvested and marketed quickly because of price fluctuation and perishability, there must be available sufficient workers to carry on peak operations.

Industrial operations using migratory-casual workers are both seasonal and intermittent in nature. The construction of highways, railroads, dams, and levees is affected both by weather conditions and the public's attitude toward construction projects. Excavations and fills must be made before the rainy season, cement must be poured before cold weather, and grading must be finished before snow falls. But the activity and the labor demand of these processes may also be influenced by public interest or indifference. Bond issues for construction projects—roads, dams, drainage canals—are frequently dependent upon the crystallization of public opinion. In some of the industries employing migratory-casual workers, notably lumbering, operating fluctuations resulting from changes in the price of the finished product are as great as those resulting from weather conditions.

Some of these industrial processes require a labor force the year around (e. g., railroad maintenance) to which additions are made at times of the year when weather or other conditions permit or require work to be done. Others (e. g., packing and preserving fruits and vegetables) operate for a part of the year with a large labor force, which is disbanded completely between seasons of activity. Still other processes (e. g., construction) are nonrecurrent; the labor demand begins and ends with the initiation and the completion of the project.

---

[9] The depression transient found a considerable proportion of his employment during migration at jobs regularly followed by the habitual migratory-casual worker. For further discussion of this point, see Webb, John N., The Transient Unemployed, Research Monograph III, Division of Social Research, Works Progress Administration, Washington, D. C., 1936, p. 54.

3. Most of the agricultural and industrial processes that depend upon a mobile labor supply are extractive operations, and, almost of necessity, they are located in areas of low population density. Such of the construction projects as are not extractive are essential links between the extraction and the fabrication of raw material, and, therefore, are more likely to be found in areas of low than in areas of high population density. The separation of economic functions geographically has determined to a large extent the present population pattern, and consequently the distribution of the labor supply. The result has been that natural and economic forces have worked together in such a way that many extractive processes are located in areas sufficiently removed from population centers to make a mobile labor supply essential to those having seasonal or intermittent peaks of activity.

These characteristics help to explain why certain agricultural and industrial processes need migratory-casual workers. Because of the marked seasonality or irregularity of their operations, none of these processes provides enough continuing employment to support an adequate resident labor force, or enough earnings to allow the workers to live on accumulated wages between seasons. Although frequently a portion of the workers needed during peak operations is drawn from the local labor supply, this source is uncertain.[10] Obviously, a surplus labor force several times the size of that regularly employed cannot exist in the sparsely settled areas, where so many of these processes are located, for the sake of a few months' seasonal employment even though the wage for seasonal work may at times exceed that for permanent employment.[11]

Efforts to overcome this difficulty through stabilization of the mobile labor reserve needed only during peak operations within a fairly restricted area have failed, and of necessity must fail, in most

---

[10] A study of farm labor in the Yakima Valley, Wash., shows that resident labor could—but does not—meet all the labor demands of the valley during the whole year, excepting only the months of September and October, the peak months of the hop and apple harvests. But, during October, the local labor supply is altogether insufficient. During the third week of October 1935, resident workers performed less than one-half of the total work done in the fruit crops. See Landis, Paul H., and Brooks, Melvin S., Farm Labor in the Yakima Valley, Wash., Rural Sociology Series in Farm Labor, no. 1, Washington State College, Pullman, Wash., 1936.

[11] Employers requiring a marked increase in the working force for seasonal operations are sometimes agreed that it would be desirable to hold these workers in the locality by finding off-season employment for them. This is particularly true of seasonal operations of longer duration, and of those in which there is likelihood that workers will not be available when needed. For example, a large sugar-beet refinery sent a letter to growers and beet workers in which it was stated that: "This company has been, and is, interested in the welfare of beet workers employed by growers who sell beets to it, not only during the period when field work is being done, but also during other parts of the year. In particular, in the past, this company has on several occasions secured work during part of the period between the end of the harvest and the beginning of thinning, on railroads and elsewhere, for beet workers." Through the Leaves, published by the Great Western Sugar Co., Denver, Colo., December 1929, vol. XVII, p. 548.

instances. Unless an area has a diversity of productive processes with seasonal peak labor demands occurring in sequence, there will not be enough employment to maintain the worker throughout the year.[12] A sequence of this kind within an area so restricted in size as to allow the worker to maintain permanent residence is rare among extractive processes, if it occurs at all.

Therefore, it seems evident that as long as resident workers do not provide the necessary labor reserve, and stabilization of mobile workers within restricted areas lacks the economic support of adequate employment sequences, seasonal and intermittent processes in agriculture and industry must employ migratory-casual workers. This raises the basic question of why these processes can continue to benefit from a large and mobile labor supply for which their responsibility is limited to a few weeks or months of employment during the year. Or, to state the same question from the point of view of the worker, why a mobile labor reserve continues to exist for the operation of these processes. From the discussion up to this point, it is plain that the answer to the question is complex. Clearly, both economic and personal factors are involved, and, although the two are closely interrelated, they must be discussed separately if their significance is to be assessed accurately.

On the economic side, the migratory-casual worker is the result of (1) the progression of the seasons which provides an irregular sequence of employment over a large area, and (2) the pool of unemployment that rises and falls with business conditions, but which is never completely drained.

The great expanse of the country, with its variety of climates and its low population density in widely separated areas of production, is a primary factor in an explanation of the continued existence of the migratory-casual worker. The size and the geography of the United States produce different climates, and, consequently, different seasons for the maturing of crops and the operation of subsidiary seasonal industries (e. g., canning), and for the initiation of construction and maintenance work.[13] Thus, over a large area there is a fairly continuous demand for workers to fill short-time jobs, each of which is inadequate to maintain a resident worker. The result is obvious. Migratory-casual workers move into these areas to supplement the local labor supply during the peak of operations, and then move on, frequently across one or more States, to find their next employment.

---

[12] See ch. IV for illustrations of pronounced overlapping of peak activities in the principal processes employing migratory-casual workers.

[13] In the Southwest, for example, construction often stops because of summertime heat; but in the rest of the country summer is the most important building season.

Important as this factor is, it provides an incomplete explanation for the existence of the migratory-casual worker. Account must also be taken of the irregularity of employment provided by industry to the urban worker, of the low wages and small opportunity offered by agriculture to the rural worker; in short, of the insecurity of life that besets the wage earner at the unskilled and semiskilled levels. Carleton Parker described the economic conditions creating the migratory-casual worker in the following words:

> The irregularity of industrial employment is as important an element as the height of the wage scale * * *. The combination of low wages, the unskilled nature of the work and its great irregularity, tends to break the habit and desire for stable industry among the workers. Millions drift into migrating from one industrial center to another in search of work * * *. The worker slides down the scale and out of his industry and joins the millions of unskilled or lost-skilled who float back and forth from Pennsylvania to Missouri and from the lumber camps to the Gulf States and California.[14]

Clearly, the way in which industry is organized and the way in which it operates have a pronounced effect on the stability of the working population. Our modern economy, by freeing the majority of the working population from attachment to the soil has, through territorial specialization, brought about great concentrations of population in the cities to perform the function of fabricating and distributing goods for consumption and production use. The growth of the working population in one of the great industrial centers may be used to illustrate this point. The United States Census of Population shows that in 1930 the number of gainful workers in the total United States was approximately one and two-thirds times as large as in 1900; but, during the same period, the number of gainful workers in Detroit had increased fivefold.

In this somewhat extreme case of labor concentration, it was a single industry—automobile manufacturing—which caused a marked migration of resident workmen because it offered greater opportunity to the worker. But the employment that caused this migration was, and is, notoriously insecure of tenure. The worker of slender means who was attracted by the high wages of the automobile factories during good times must move again when work is slack. In this constant attempt at adjustment of labor supply to demand it is not surprising that a body of habitual migrants is created. This process was succinctly described by a witness during hearings before the Commission on Industrial Relations in 1914:

---

[14] Parker, Carleton, The Casual Laborer and Other Essays, Harcourt, Brace & Co., New York, 1920, p. 119.

Mr. Page [a lumber mill owner]: "I think the more a man roves, the more he wants to rove. And I do not think it is the seasonal work that causes the roving * * *. I think that the cause is that you have got 15 jobs and 16 men." [15]

It is this failure to achieve a balance of workers and jobs that creates the labor surplus, or pool of unemployment, which has become a permanent feature of modern economic organization. It might seem that recognition of the social loss resulting from the surplus would have led to a search for remedial action. Such has not been the case in the past, and for good reason. A surplus labor supply is profitable to the employer, and particularly to the employer whose labor force must be materially augmented because of recurring or intermittent peak operations.

An oversupply of migratory-casual workers keeps the wage rate low, permits some selection of the working force, provides immediate replacements for those who leave before the work is done, and operates as a check on the organization of workers to improve working conditions. [16] Not only do employers favor the existence of a surplus labor force but frequently they also assist in creating this surplus through advertisements for workers, broadcast in the newspapers of their own and neighboring States. Attempts have been made, and are now being made, to reduce the oversupply of workers through proper direction of the existing labor force into areas of demand. But, as the following excerpt suggests, such attempts meet with difficulties:

> The Oregon Department of Labor has estimated that we have enough workers now resident in the State to harvest all our crops, if these workers were properly mobilized in the direction where needed * * *. But it is a slow process to persuade some of our agricultural employers that they do not need a large surplus of floating labor in order to establish a reasonable wage scale. [17]

In the interest of maintaining a plentiful supply of migratory-casual worker for seasonal employment, immigrant labor, particularly Oriental and Mexican, has been extensively imported. The superficial advantages of these auxiliaries are obvious. The ob-

---

[15] Report of the Commission on Industrial Relations, S. Doc. No. 415, 64th Cong., Washington, D. C., 1916, vol. V, p. 4252.

[16] Working and living conditions are generally poor even where a State inspection system is maintained. For instance: Only 20 percent of the labor camps inspected in California during 1933-34 were rated "good" by the Supervisor of Camp Inspection. Over a period of 20 years less than 30 percent were rated "good." Migratory Labor in California, op. cit., p. 78.

Where no inspection or supervision is maintained, the only force operating to improve poor conditions is the refusal of workers to accept employment, resulting in unusually high labor turnover.

[17] See Problem of the Automobile "Floater", op. cit., p. 13.

jective in each case was a cheap, industrious, and tractable labor supply as a supplement to the more expensive and incalculable white worker. First the Chinese, then the Japanese, and finally the Mexican laborer has been recruited for work in the mines, on the railroads, in the orchards, and in the fields. A discussion of the relative merits of Chinese and Japanese workers during a convention of employers was the occasion for the following statement:

> The Chinese when they were here were ideal. They were patient, plodding, and uncomplaining in the performance of the most menial service. They submitted to anything, never violating a contract. The exclusion acts drove them out. The Japanese now [1907] coming in are a tricky and cunning lot, who break contracts and become quite independent. They are not organized into unions, but their clannishness seems to operate as a union would. One trick is to contract work at a certain price and then in the rush of the harvest, threaten to strike unless wages are raised.[18]

When immigration restrictions stopped the influx of Oriental workers, the Mexican, free from such restrictions, began to constitute an increasingly important element in the labor forces of railroad construction and maintenance, mining, and agriculture; in fact, in precisely those industries that depend upon a plentiful supply of mobile workers for unskilled jobs. If Mexican labor proved to be less industrious than Chinese or Japanese, it was easy to handle, cheap, and plentiful in supply. During the hearings on a bill in Congress to restrict immigration from Mexico, a representative from the Fresno, Calif., Chamber of Commerce testified:

> The Mexican is not aggressive * * *. He does not take the Chinese and Japanese attitude. He is a fellow easy to handle * * * a man who gives us no trouble at all * * * He takes his orders and follows them * * *.[19]

It should be apparent that the employer's interest in a plentiful labor supply is twofold: He desires a mobile labor reserve large enough to handle peak operations and a labor supply that must accept low wages, long hours, and poor working conditions without effective protest. These interests have been furthered by the importation of cheap foreign labor. The pressure on the labor market exerted by the availability of this low-standard labor supply is probably much in excess of the actual numbers competing with the native migratory-casual worker; but the desired effect is achieved,

---

[18] California Fruit Growers' Convention Proceedings, 1907, quoted in Migratory Labor in California, op. cit., p. 22.

[19] Testimony of Frisselle, S. Parker, "Seasonal Agricultural Laborers from Mexico", Hearings Before the Committee on Immigration and Naturalization, 69th Cong., 1st sess., Washington, D. C., 1926.

and when occasion demands, labor recruiting offices are ready to supply the cheap labor necessary to the maintenance of a low wage level. The strong economic bias in the employer's attitude toward the source of a low-wage labor supply is shown by the repeated statement of preference for white migratory-casual workers qualified by the complaint that the white worker, and especially the native white, is undependable as a worker and intractable as a person.[20]

The advantages that the employer derives from a large and mobile labor supply are frequently more apparent than real. Against them must be set a number of serious disadvantages, some of which are restricted in effect to employers, while others are felt by entire communities. Irregular employment and low earnings leave the migratory-casual worker with small reserves to carry him through periods of unemployment that even in good years covers a considerable portion of his working year. The result is an expenditure for relief that in effect represents a public and private subsidy to seasonal and intermittent industries. The lower the wage level, the higher the public cost. For instance, a field report on migratory-casual clam diggers in the vicinity of Gray's Harbor, Washington, states in part:

> The supervisors of the relief agencies in Aberdeen and Hoquiam, Wash., were distressed over the chaotic condition of this industry (clam canneries), both from the client's point of view and from their own, in the problem of administering relief fairly. In Aberdeen the experienced clam diggers had been told in advance that their relief cases would be closed while they were digging. Figures taken from the books of one of the canneries showed that a majority of the diggers earned between $15 and $30 per month. Most of the diggers were, of course, relief recipients, and, therefore, relief grants amount to a subsidization of the industry. No pressure could be brought on this point, because clam digging is not "full time" employment, because clam diggers can work only during minus tides.[21]

Another disadvantage of maintaining a large labor surplus is the cost of recruiting workers willing to accept the wages and working conditions offered. On this point the Mexican migratory-casual worker offers the only case from which definite evidence of recruiting costs can be drawn. The average cost of recruiting and shipping a worker was, according to a study of Mexican labor, $28 in 1920,

---

[20] "White cotton pickers were generally and frankly not wanted in Nueces County, Tex. [typical cotton region]. Farmers stated: 'People here don't want white pickers. They prefer Mexicans; they are content with whatever you give them. The whites want more water, etc., and are trouble makers. If there is a labor shortage they want exorbitant prices * * * you can handle the Mexicans better; they're more subservient * * *.' " Taylor, Paul S., An American Mexican Frontier, University of North Carolina Press, Chapel Hill, N. C., 1934, p. 130.

[21] Excerpt from a field report of one of the interviewers on the study of migratory-casual workers.

of which "about 15 percent was spent in soliciting * * * and
85 percent was used for railroad fares and food [en route]." [22]

More important than these, in some respects, are two basic disadvantages which are inherent in a migratory-casual labor supply
that is both too large and has little or no direction: (1) The labor
turnover is extremely high, even on jobs of short duration; and
(2) there is frequent strife between worker and employer that
promises to increase rather than decrease in bitterness.

Without an actual or potential oversupply of workers, the low
earnings, long hours, and poor working conditions of the migratory-
casual worker could not be maintained.   As long as these conditions
exist, there is no incentive for the worker to remain on one job longer
than his immediate needs require.   By leaving the job in accordance
with such personal dictates as the amount of his earnings, the difficulty of the work, or his plans for the immediate future, the migratory-casual worker has gained a reputation for instability and unre-
liability that is not fully merited.   Quitting a job before it is completed is the only peaceful protest that the worker has, and this type
of protest makes a large contribution to the high labor turnover
that is characteristic of industries dependent upon a migratory-
casual labor force.

At times, and with growing frequency in recent years, the protest
of the migratory-casual workers against wages and working conditions has led to open violence.   Unfortunately, these outbreaks have
been the only means of focusing public attention on the position of
the migratory-casual worker in the economic order.   The Wheatland
(Calif.) riots [23] of 1914, dramatized by Carleton Parker in his study
of the casual laborer, were the forerunner of the bitter conflicts that
have occurred throughout the regions of intensive crop cultivation
in the United States, especially in the San Joaquin, Imperial, and
Salinas Valleys [24] in recent years.   Concerted action by the workers
is met by armed and deputized citizenry, with the issue changing
gradually from spontaneous protest over substandard wages, poor

[22] Taylor, Paul S., Mexican Labor in the United States, Valley of the South Platte,
Colorado, University of California Publication in Economics, Berkeley, Calif., 1930, vol. I,
no. 2, p. 133.

[23] The Wheatland riots were a result of the vicious policy of recruiting unneeded
workers to keep wages down, mentioned on p. 12. "The Commission of Immigration
and Housing went to Wheatland and studied the situation. It brought to light the
following conditions: overcongestion of the camps, due to the owner's (a certain Mr.
Durst) advertising for and obtaining twice as many people for his hop harvest than
he needed, so as to be able to depress wages * * * women and children sleeping in
the fields for lack of accommodations * * * insufficient toilets (9 for 2,800 people) * * * ." Migratory Labor in California, op. cit., p. 56.

[24] George P. West, writing of the background of the strike of the lettuce packers in
Salinas, Calif., in the New York Times of Sept. 20, 1936, states: "The capitalists * * *
from the Imperial Valley [who started large-scale lettuce raising in Salinas] brought with
them an attitude toward labor developed by the handling of Mexican peons."

For an excellent summary of these conflicts, see Taylor, Paul S., and Kerr, Clark,
Uprisings on the Farms, Survey Graphic, January 1935.

working conditions, and unsanitary living quarters, to the right to organize for the purpose of collective bargaining.[25]

An excess of workers beyond actual need may be expected as long as employers of migratory-casual workers continue to hold that the advantages of an oversupply of labor outweigh the disadvantages of high labor turnover, uncertain quality of work, and occasional strife. In the past, at least, this attitude has been maintained without arousing an effective protest from the worker. The only practicable method by which the migratory-casual worker can control the supply and improve his position in the labor market appears to be organization—and organization of the migratory-casual worker has made slow progress for obvious reasons.

The migratory-casual worker is an individualist and is inclined to be impatient of the slow process of organization and negotiation that has characterized successful union policy in this country. Moreover, the migratory-casual worker lacks the basic qualifications for either the craft or the industrial type of organization because he can claim neither skilled trade nor an attachment to a particular industry. The high mobility of the migratory-casual worker makes the unification and expression of group opinion extremely difficult; and low yearly earnings make the collection of dues[26] and the building of a war chest a difficult matter. It is indicative of the nature of the migratory-casual worker and of his position in the labor market that the "one big union" type of organization, exemplified in this country by the I.W.W., has, until recent years, provided the only important evidence of susceptibility to organization. The militancy of the I.W.W., its loose organization, and its insistence upon the common cause of labor as against the narrower craft union concept appealed to the migratory-casual worker where other types of union activity failed.

---

[25] In California in 1933 there were 37 agricultural strikes, involving 47,575 workers, and affecting nearly every major crop. The strikes were chiefly against the low prevailing wage of 15 cents per hour, but other demands were pressed for recognition of the unions, and for abolition of the contract system and other unsatisfactory working conditions. See Hearings Before the Committee on Labor, House of Representatives, on H. R. 6288, 74th Cong., 1st sess., Washington, D. C., 1935, p. 342 ff.

For an interesting historical account of labor disturbences in California involving migratory-casual workers, see Migratory Labor in California, op. cit., ch. V.

[26] The difficulty of dues collection from migratory workers is probably one of the chief reasons why they have never been organized by old-line labor leaders. Migratory Labor in California (op. cit., p. 69) quotes Paul Scharrenberg, former secretary of the California State Federation of Labor as saying: "The California Federation of Labor has proved * * * to its own satisfaction that they could organize the migratory. The problem has not been to organize him but to keep him organized. * * * It is due * * * to the inability of the migratory to furnish his own funds for his organization. * * * Another problem * * * is * * * that being so underpaid and being so ignorant he falls an easy prey to radicals that have in the past defamed the A. F. of L. and kept alive a distrust for the A. F. of L. Any money invested in union dues with the A. F. of L., the migratory was told, was a bad investment. The migratory has often believed this." The study comments: "This analysis by Mr. Scharrenberg omits to state that the California Federation of Labor kept never more than two organizers in the field, and since the end of the war, none."

Up to this point, the discussion of reasons for the existence of a mobile labor supply has been almost entirely in terms of the economic factors—irregularity of employment, sharp seasonal peaks in the demand for unskilled and semiskilled labor, an unorganized and highly competitive labor market. Although economic factors are undoubtedly of primary importance, purely personal factors, such as a predilection for new scenes, new faces, short-time employment, and freedom from the restraints of community life play an important role in the creation and in the continued existence of the migratory-casual labor supply. Perhaps this point may be sharpened by a single consideration. If the economic factors are considered alone, and the personal aspects of the migratory workers assumed to be those of the average workmen, there is provided at best only a partial explanation of the migratory-casual worker. Low wages, irregular employment, and an overcrowded labor market are more nearly the rule than the exception for millions of urban and rural workers at unskilled and semiskilled pursuits, without at any time causing them to become migratory-casual workers. Something in addition to adverse economic conditions is needed to create a migratory population; and here the experience of the past few years is instructive. During the depression period the insecurity of urban workers and the insecurity plus the lack of opportunity among rural workers created a problem of unemployment relief that was essentially resident, rather than nonresident in nature.[27] Despite the pressure of economic circumstances, only a small portion of the needy unemployed turned to migration for a solution of their problem. Thus, there was a highly selective factor at work that determined who should migrate and who should not. In this respect, there is a close analogy between the temporary transient of the depression period and the habitual migratory-casual worker who is found on the road in good times and bad.

This selective factor resides in the individual and in his relationship to society. It is the result of mental processes and emotional reactions that do not lend themselves to ready description, but the net result is a distinguishing characteristic of the migratory-casual worker that can be observed and is known to those in close contact with this part of the labor supply. Almost of necessity, the employer knows these purely personal traits, and it is of interest to see the migratory-casual worker from the employer's point of view.

---

[27] The peak in resident relief occurred in January 1935 when something over 20,000,000 persons received some public assistance. The peak in transient relief occurred in February 1935 when the midmonthly census reported 300,460 persons under care. See the Monthly Report, Federal Emergency Relief Administration, Washington, D. C., December 1935, p. 79.

In the Wenatchee Valley, Wash., the migratory-casual worker is a well-known figure and an essential supplement to the local labor supply when the principal crop—apples—is harvested. An observing employer has provided this description of the migratory-casual worker:

> The wanderers around Wenatchee are a jumble. Many are newcomers on the scene. Many have swung around a wide circle of scenes, occupations, and climes so many times that they have completely lost the count. Jake Williams, from Indiana, was picking apples with me 2 years ago. He was then on either the third or fourth lap of a fairly uniform circuit—and last year he was back for another lap of the same. As the apple-picking season would close he would head for Phoenix, Ariz., riding the box cars and figuring out his schedules with the precision of Vincent Astor or Henry Ford. "I like Phoenix", he said—"clothes are such a small problem there. And do you know", he casually observed, "we have now developed to the point where we can call up almost any yardmaster in the country and learn with precision, almost to the minute, when the next through drag [freight] will be going our way."
>
> Jake stayed at Phoenix awhile and then he moved on East, varying his route more or less for change of scene and companionship. He had a sister in Chicago and so he dropped in at her home for awhile. He had another sister in Brooklyn and he always had to see her on his rounds. He roamed over a wide country, simply drifting along. He had nothing especially in view except to move along. The railroads carried him free, so why stop very long? Presently a bright and annual thought came to him very suddenly—why, hell, apple picking will come on at Wenatchee next month, so why stay in the East? The red apples are beckoning to him 2,000 miles or so away, but their beckoning is strong, he needs a change of exercise and food, and he needs to complete his circuit, and so here he comes again and again.
>
> Jake may have worked a little in the wheat fields and with the oranges, but, so far as I could learn, he mostly roamed, picked apples, and roamed again. I would not be sure (nor would he), but I think he was unmarried.[28]

This worker may seem, from the employer's description, a little too carefree, irresponsible, and lacking in a definite social attitude toward the work he does and the men he works for. The same employer, with a nice sense of contrast, reports on "New York Harry":

> He claimed to have come from Syracuse, N. Y., in the Finger Lakes district, where many apples are raised. He had roamed widely and came to us fresh from the Yakima, Wash., hop fields, where I am sure he played many tricks and weighed in much dirt. [Note.—Hop picking is paid by the pound.] His philosophy was summed up in one advisory statement: "The * * * won't pay you anything for what you do, and the only chance to get anywhere is to pick (hops, apples, etc.) 'em dirty, limbs and all." [28]

---

[28] Excerpts from a letter in the files of the Division of Social Research, Works Progress Administration, Washington, D. C.

Where one employer is able to understand something of the personal factor in the migratory-casual worker, there are many more who do not understand. To this large group, migratory-casual workers are "a disparate group of misfits, bitten by wanderlust." The employer disapproves of the migratory-casual worker's independence both for economic reasons and because it seems to be an open contradiction of the adage that independence is earned by thrift and industry. The employer resents the thinly-veiled hostility of the worker and, more often than not, fails utterly to understand the reason for the constant and profitless roving about the country. For that matter, it is doubtful if the migratory-casual worker himself knows just what it is that drives him on.

A study of the labor supply in the wheat belt found that the migratory-casual worker was inclined to be vague about the reasons for his way of life:

> Asked why he has come to the harvest, the seasoned "floater" probably will answer that "the harvest is a habit", [sic] that he swears each year he will never come again, but cannot seem to resist when the time comes. It fascinates him with its multitudes, its unknown possibilities, its chance that "something may turn up." [29]

Occasionally, a migratory-casual worker has both the urge and the ability to write for publication what he believes to be the reasons for his continued wandering. Unfortunately, when the migratory-casual worker becomes literate, he usually becomes romantic.

> With each experience, the fascination of fruit tramping increases, for it includes travel, change, new scenes, fresh faces, different food, and good money. Mickey [his wife] and I have become typical. We hate the small-town idea of doing the average thing, and we do not want a house and lot. I don't believe anyone really does. It's just something real-estate men sell to you. [30]

The romanticized interpretation of the personal factors in the making of a migratory-casual worker is easily and frequently overdone by observers as well as by the worker himself. And yet this interpretation cannot be dismissed as having no claim for attention. The hard and objective facts of irregular employment before migration, of a gradual shift from haphazard search for steady employment to a regular pattern of migration, of a lessening of ambition and a lack of interest in saving for the future—all these fail to explain the personal factor adequately. Something else is needed to make the explanation complete. Perhaps it can only be said that it is essential to the migratory-casual worker that he move, that no one environ-

---

[29] Lescohier, Don D., Harvest Labor Problems in the Wheat Belt, Bulletin 1020, U. S. Department of Agriculture, Washington, D. C., 1922, p. 18.
[30] Whitaker, P. W., "Fruit Tramps", Century Magazine, March 1929.

ment claim him for long, that scenes be new and persons different. These desires, expressed or only vaguely felt, are the core of his existence and the governor of his activity. The work he does is a means to this end; the industries dependent upon his labor are conveniently dispersed. In an economic sense these industries make his existence possible and influence his social attitudes, but in a personal sense he holds himself to be independent of them.

It is this real or fancied independence that has done much to make a romantic figure of the migratory-casual worker. For many of those who have felt the urge to break the routine of monotonous tasks, to throw aside the cautions of thrift and industry, and to take to the road in order to prove to themselves and to the world that they are in fact free agents, the migratory-casual worker is an attractive figure. He is admired but not entirely approved; and he is known not as he is but as he is reported in fiction and legend. The migratory-casual worker in the character of the lumberjack is the hero of the woods, and his great deeds have been the theme of folklore and story of which "the legend of Paul Bunyan is certainly the greatest of these creations; for it embodies the souls of the millions of American camp men who have always done the hard and perilous pioneer labor of this country." [31]

Another well-known legend of the migratory-casual worker is even more authentic folklore than the Bunyan legend. Strangely enough, it is the legend of the Negro migratory-casual worker—the roustabout, the cotton picker, the levee worker, and the railroad and tunnel construction laborer. It is the legend of the Negro John Henry, who was "six feet tall, didn't know his own stren'th", but could carry three bales of cotton, one on his head and one on either shoulder. He was "big and black and mean and his feet didn't touch de ground—and his home wasn't hyar. His foots was always itchin'!" [32]

The hold that these and similar legends have upon the imagination of a restless nation is no accident. These legends grew up around the "deacon's seat" in the bunkhouses of the logging camps, around the campfires in the fields, in the mining camps, and along the railroad right-of-way. The stories were told by migratory-casual workers to dramatize their lives, and these stories are often remarkably accurate portrayals of the inward urge to be ever on the move.

---

[31] Stevens, James, Paul Bunyan, Alfred A., Knopf, Inc., New York, 1925. See also Shephard, Esther, Paul Bunyan (revised edition), Harcourt, Brace & Co., New York, 1925.

[32] Bradford, Roark, John Henry, Harper & Bros., New York, 1931. One of the legends not included in the Bradford account, but widely held to be the original, is that John Henry was a tunnel worker on the B. & O. Railroad.

But there is another, and darker, side to the life of the migratory-casual worker. Old age has little but trouble in store for him. When younger, he was a better and more dependable workman; age dulls his skill and sharpens his individualistic and, frequently, his antisocial tendencies. He has no prospects for the future, and by the time he has reached middle age has most likely ceased to worry about them. In most cases, long before he is 60, age will have permanently removed him from the labor market. Disease or the hardships of his life will have taken their toll of his strength. He will then almost certainly become a permanent charge on some community, as a "park bum", as an inmate of a hospital, asylum, or jail, or as a panhandler on the street for money to buy cheap liquor and a little food.

At this point the discussion quits the general approach and turns to an analysis of the 500 work histories that have been assembled. The concern of the discussion hereafter shall be to examine some of the measurable attributes of migratory-casual workers reported for the 500 workers and to clarify, in terms of their concrete manifestations, the general forces that have been described. Succeeding chapters, for example, will describe numerically such aspects as seasonal fluctuation in employment, duration of individual jobs, the labor demand of the crops and processes in which the workers were employed, time spent yearly in employment, and the amount of earnings. Chapter II, beginning this description with an account of the geography of the migrations of the 500 workers, deals with the distances they traveled, the paths beaten by their migrations, and the States in which they obtained the most work.

EXTENT OF MIGRATION

IN THE COURSE of a year a migratory-casual worker may cross the continent and return, or he may remain within the limits of a few contiguous counties in one State. The extent of his migration during any year depends upon the migratory-work pattern that he has developed, the employment conditions in the industry or industries that make this employment sequence possible, and his disposition toward work and travel.

In measuring and portraying the extent of migration, two methods have been employed: (1) a quantitative statement of the number of State-line crossings during the migratory period in each of 2 years—1933 and 1934;·and (2) a graphic statement in the form of a series of maps showing the itineraries of a number of migratory-casual workers during the 2 years combined. The purpose of the maps is to supplement and illustrate the tabular data on extent of migration and to show the migratory-work patterns that are peculiar to several important productive processes.

NUMERICAL STATEMENT

Interstate migration was the rule among the 500 workers included in this study (see table 1). By using the device of counting State-line crossings reported in the actual employment records of these workers, it was found that in each of the 2 years, 1933 and 1934, about two-thirds of them crossed at least one State line and one-fourth crossed at least six State lines. In weighing the value of this information as a measure of extent of migration, it must be remembered that the data represent the crossing of State lines rather than State areas.

Although a substantial majority of the 500 migratory-casual workers crossed 1 or more State lines during each of the 2 years, there were enough workers who remained within the borders of 1 State to deserve comment. The 1933 work histories showed that somewhat less than one-third of the workers had not been outside the borders of one State, and the 1934 work histories showed this to be true of about one-fifth of the workers (see table 1). The nature of these strictly intrastate migratory-work patterns is clearly evident in the vicinity of Seattle, Minneapolis, and Memphis on the illustrative maps to be discussed later (see figs. 1, 2, and 3).

The Migratory-Casual Worker

TABLE 1.—NUMBER OF STATE-LINE CROSSINGS OF 500 MIGRATORY-CASUAL WORKERS, 1933–34

Number of State-line crossings	1933				1934			
	Total	Type of worker			Total	Type of worker		
		Agricultural	Industrial	Combination [1]		Agricultural	Industrial	Combination [1]
All workers	500	200	100	200	500	200	100	200
	Percent distribution							
All workers	100	100	100	100	100	100	100	100
No State line	29	31	31	27	20	27	19	15
1 State line	7	6	7	7	8	6	11	8
2 State lines	15	13	16	17	12	10	15	12
3 State lines	7	7	8	6	7	6	3	9
4 State lines	7	6	9	8	8	8	6	7
5 State lines	4	6	1	4	5	5	4	6
6 to 10 State lines	13	12	13	12	18	19	20	15
11 to 15 State lines	6	8	4	5	11	12	15	9
16 to 20 State lines	4	5	6	2	3	3	1	5
21 to 25 State lines	1	2		1	1	2	2	
26 to 30 State lines	1	1	1		(2)	(2)		(2)
31 to 35 State lines	(2)	(2)						
Not ascertainable	6	3	4	11	7	2	4	14

[1] Workers combining agricultural and industrial employment.
[2] Less than 0.5 percent.

In contrast to the restricted movements of intrastate migrants was the extensive movement of 11 to 15 percent of the 500 workers whose employment histories show that they crossed 11 to 25 State lines. Between these 2 extremes—no State-line crossings and 11 or more—are to be found over one-half of the 500 workers. Thus, interstate migration appears to be a clearly defined characteristic of the migratory-casual worker.

In 1933 the three types of workers [1]—agricultural, principally industrial, and combination agricultural and industrial—were, in terms of State-line crossings, about equally mobile (see table 1). A similar examination for the year 1934 shows that agricultural workers were somewhat less mobile in terms of State-line crossings than were the other two types. On this point the evidence is clearer on the maps showing the itineraries of agricultural and of principally industrial workers for the 2 years combined.

---

[1] Type of worker was determined from the history of employment during the 2 years. Workers following agricultural employment solely during the 2 years, or having only occasional nonagricultural jobs, were classified as agricultural workers. The same procedure was followed for the industrial group, although there were fewer workers reporting solely industrial employment. The third group—agricultural and industrial—represents workers whose employment during the 2 years was divided so equally between agriculture and industry that a combination type was the only logical classification. In the interest of brevity and convenience, the three groups will frequently be referred to simply as *agricultural, industrial,* and *combination workers.*

Although any conclusions concerning the relative extent of migration among the three types of workers must, on the evidence presented in table 1, be tentative, there are logical reasons for expecting the migration of agricultural workers to be less extensive than that of industrial workers and of workers following both kinds of employment. Extent of migration is determined in large part by the sequence of employment which the worker knows by experience to be possible. The time consumed in travel from job to job during the working season represents a loss to the worker. Efforts to minimize this loss would naturally tend to restrict the extent of migration to the smallest area in which a satisfactory job sequence could be obtained.

Agriculture provides the migratory-casual worker with greater opportunity for employment sequences within restricted areas than does industry. The agricultural worker in the Middle West may harvest grain in a number of places in the same State and then double back for plowing as the season progresses. California boasts that within her borders a crop matures in each month of the year. Under favorable crop and employment conditions, a few of the more fortunate migratory-casual workers in that State might begin the year picking or packing citrus fruits, go on to work in the vegetable, berry, grain, and hop fields, pick deciduous fruits, or cotton, and return to the citrus groves again with no longer periods of unemployment than the time required to move from one crop area to another. By extending the range of migration to adjoining States to take advantage of the variety of climates and diversified crops, the agricultural migratory-casual worker can, and often does, establish a migratory-work pattern which he follows year after year with a fair degree of assurance that employment will be found.

Analogous situations are less frequent among the industrial processes that employ migratory-casual labor. The completion of a dam or road construction project may necessitate considerable travel to the site of another project, or may require travel to several projects before employment is secured. Moreover, in industrial processes there is less of the regularly recurring employment that follows from the progression of the seasons.

It would seem, therefore, that insofar as the extent of migration is a direct result of an established migratory-work pattern, the migratory-casual worker in industry would find it necessary to travel over a larger area than the agricultural worker. Furthermore, it seems logical to expect that migratory-casual workers lacking an established work pattern would have the greater extent of migration since chance and rumor would be important factors in determining the direction of their travels. Chance and rumor were found to be important

factors in the wanderings of depression transients [2] whose employment during migration was both casual and noncasual in nature, and
included both agricultural and industrial pursuits. Reference to
table 1 shows that among 200 migratory-casual workers following
a combination of agricultural and industrial employments during
both 1933 and 1934, there was a smaller proportion of intrastate migrants than among either the agricultural or industrial types. Further evidence on the relative extent of migration by type of workers
will be presented in connection with the discussion of selected
itineraries.

TABLE 2.—NUMBER OF STATES IN WHICH EMPLOYMENT WAS OBTAINED
DURING MIGRATION BY 500 MIGRATORY-CASUAL WORKERS, 1933–34

Number of States in which employed	1933				1934			
	Total	Type of worker			Total	Type of worker		
		Agricultural	Industrial	Combination [1]		Agricultural	Industrial	Combination [1]
All workers	500	200	100	200	500	200	100	200
	Percent distribution							
All workers	100	100	100	100	100	100	100	100
No State [2]	5	4	4	6	4	5	2	6
1 State	55	57	59	51	54	58	52	50
2 States	27	24	26	30	28	24	31	31
3 States	8	10	6	8	9	9	11	8
4 States	3	4	4	1	3	3	2	2
5 to 8 States	1	1		2	1	1	1	1
Not ascertainable	1	(3)	1	2	1		1	2

[1] Workers combining agricultural and industrial employment.
[2] I. e., workers unemployed.
[3] Less than 0.5 percent.

The fact that migratory-casual workers crossed a specified number
of State lines during the year provides no information on their
success in finding employment during migration.[3] An investigation
of this point (see table 2) shows that the number of States in which
migratory-casual workers obtained employment during each of the
2 years was in sharp contrast to the number of State-line crossings
during these years (see table 1). Somewhat over one-half of the 500
workers were employed in only 1 State and an additional one-quarter
in only 2 States, whereas about one-half of the workers had crossed
1 to 10 State lines and 11 to 15 percent had crossed 11 to 25 State
lines during the migratory period of 1 year.

---

[2] See Webb, John N., The Transient Unemployed, Research Monograph III, Division of
Social Research, Works Progress Administration, Washington, D. C., 1936, p. 54.
[3] For the number of jobs obtained during migration, see table 5, p. 56.

A comparison of the number of State-line crossings with the number of States in which employment was obtained indicates that much of the travel reported by these workers did not result in employment, but was for the express purpose of getting to or from areas in which their labor might be in demand. There are two factors which help to explain this result: (1) The established work pattern of the experienced migratory-casual worker includes more than one possibility of employment so that when no work is to be had in an area there is at least one alternative possibility in another area that can be acted upon immediately; and (2) it is known that many of the confirmed migratory-casual workers congregate in such cities as Seattle, Minneapolis, and Chicago during their off-seasons, and winter headquarters are frequently at a considerable distance from the area in which they were employed during the working season. Whenever either or both of these factors are operative, the extent of migration as measured by State-line crossings is increased relative to the number of States in which employment is secured.

Further examination of the data in table 2 shows that in 1933 there was little difference among the two types of workers—agricultural and industrial—in respect to the number of States in which employment was obtained. In 1934, however, the proportion of agricultural workers employed in only one State was distinctly larger than was true of the other two types. Here, as in the discussion of State-line crossings, the more compact migratory-work patterns of agricultural employment have a direct bearing. The data on number of States in which employed tend to support the conclusion that the migration of agricultural workers is more restricted than is that of industrial workers and workers following a combination of the two types of employment.

GRAPHIC STATEMENT

Measurement of extent of migration in terms of State-line crossings clearly establishes the interstate character of the migratory-casual worker; but this device does not disclose the patterns of migration that are developed. In order to show this important characteristic, a series of maps has been prepared from the itineraries of a selected number of the migratory-casual workers included in this study. For the purpose of discussion these maps of routes of travel during employment are grouped as follows: (1) the routes—without distinction as to type of crop—of migratory-casual workers following agricultural employment; and—without distinction as to type of processes—of workers following industrial employment; (2) the routes of agricultural workers employed principally in five important crops; and (3) the routes of industrial workers employed principally in five important industrial processes.

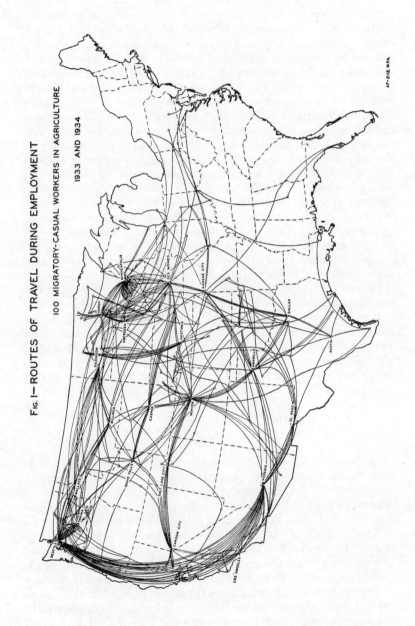

FIG. I—ROUTES OF TRAVEL DURING EMPLOYMENT

100 MIGRATORY-CASUAL WORKERS IN AGRICULTURE

1933 AND 1934

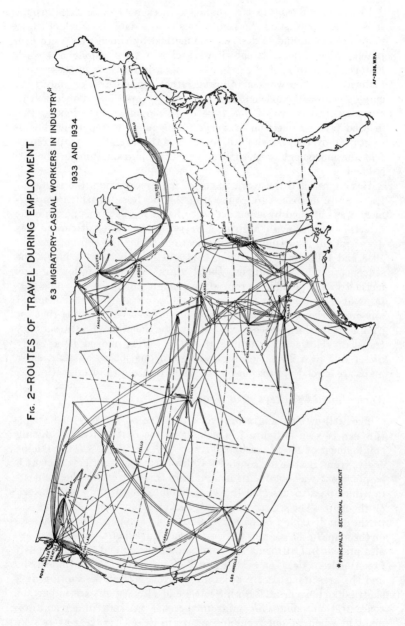

FIG. 2–ROUTES OF TRAVEL DURING EMPLOYMENT

63 MIGRATORY-CASUAL WORKERS IN INDUSTRY*

1933 AND 1934

* PRINCIPALLY SECTIONAL MOVEMENT

Before considering briefly the maps in each of these three groups it is necessary to state the limitations of the data upon which these maps are based, and to describe the method by which they were prepared. The itineraries shown were chosen from among 500 work histories available; choice was based upon indications in these work histories that the worker followed either agricultural or industrial employment with sufficient regularity to permit using his work itinerary as illustrative of one type of employment. Obviously, this method favored selection of workers who found employment during migration over those who did not, and to this extent the maps represent the movement of the more successful migrants among the 500 studied.

Having selected the work histories for presentation, the routes of travel were described by connecting the locations in which employment was obtained by smoothed lines following as far as possible the direction of the main highways or railroads. Each itinerary was drawn in full, starting with the location of the first job obtained in 1933 and following throughout 1933 and 1934, without a break, the sequence of the jobs during the 2 years. Only by following this method was it possible to reproduce enough itineraries to define patterns of migration. It is seldom possible to trace the movements of any one worker on the maps; nor would it be correct to insist that the composite patterns necessarily follow the identical routes actually traveled. However, assuming that the worker moved in a fairly direct line by railroad or highway from one job to another, these maps are a good approximation of the actual routes of migration.

Agricultural Workers as a Group.

The well-defined migratory-work patterns of workers in agriculture can be seen in figure 1, which shows the routes of travel during employment of 100 of these workers in 1933 and 1934. On the Pacific coast, from Seattle to southern California, the locations in which employment was obtained form clusters through which the connecting lines pass to describe the most definite interstate work pattern on the map. The strictly intrastate movements which were disclosed by the data in table 1 on page 24 and in table 2 on page 26 are best seen on the maps in the vicinity of Seattle and Minneapolis, though they are also present in California between San Francisco and the environs of Los Angeles. Between Seattle and Yakima, and between Minneapolis and the area immediately adjacent, there is a clear description of a shuttle-like movement. Both Seattle and Minneapolis are important concentration points for migratory-casual workers in agriculture, many of whom go out from and return to these cities year after year with only occasional trips outside the States in which these cities are located. An interesting interstate pattern that involves four State-line crossings but is still restricted in extent is to be found in the elliptical cluster of lines connecting Minneapolis, Minn., Fargo, N. Dak., Aberdeen, S. Dak., and Des Moines, Iowa.

Industrial Workers as a Group.

In contrast with the relatively compact migratory-work patterns of agricultural workers, shown in figure 1, are the dispersed patterns of industrial workers, shown in figures 2 and 3. In fact, an attempt to present 100 itineraries of industrial workers on one map resulted in such a confusion of lines that patterns could not be distinguished at all. For this reason the itineraries were divided into two groups: those in which the routes of travel were restricted to sectional movements (fig. 2), and those in which the movements were both sectional and transcontinental (fig. 3).

Strictly intrastate work patterns among industrial migratory-casual workers are to be seen in figures 2 and 3 in the vicinity of Seattle, Denver, and Dallas. When these restricted patterns are excluded it is immediately apparent that the locations in which employment was obtained by industrial workers are much more dispersed than those of agricultural workers. Even if the itineraries shown in figures 2 and 3 were combined in one map, there still would be no such cluster of job locations as that found for agricultural workers along the Pacific coast in figure 1.

The impression gained from a study of the itineraries of industrial workers is that there was less retracing of the same routes and greater distances between stops than was found in the itineraries of agricultural workers. Thus, if agricultural and industrial workers are to be compared in respect to extent of migration, the device of measuring State-line crossings needs to be supplemented by maps in order to determine the distances traveled. For example, the movement between San Francisco and Salt Lake City involves two State-line crossings, and yet the extent of migration is less than that between Los Angeles and Portland (Oreg.) (see fig. 3), which only involves one State-line crossing. On the basis of the evidence in figures 1, 2, and 3, and in view of the logical considerations advanced on page 25 it may be said that work patterns of migratory-casual workers in agriculture are not only more clearly defined but are also more restricted in extent than are work patterns of industrial workers.

No attempt was made in preparing figures 1, 2, and 3 to differentiate routes of travel among agricultural or industrial workers according to the crop or process that provided employment during migration. The purpose of this first group of maps was to show

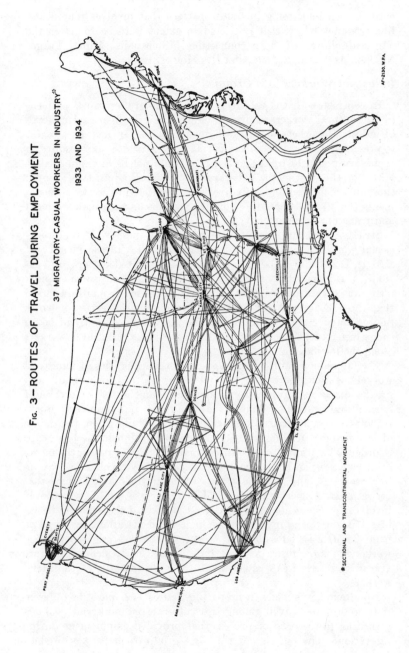

FIG. 3—ROUTES OF TRAVEL DURING EMPLOYMENT

37 MIGRATORY-CASUAL WORKERS IN INDUSTRY*

1933 AND 1934

*SECTIONAL AND TRANSCONTINENTAL MOVEMENT

AF-2130. W.P.A.

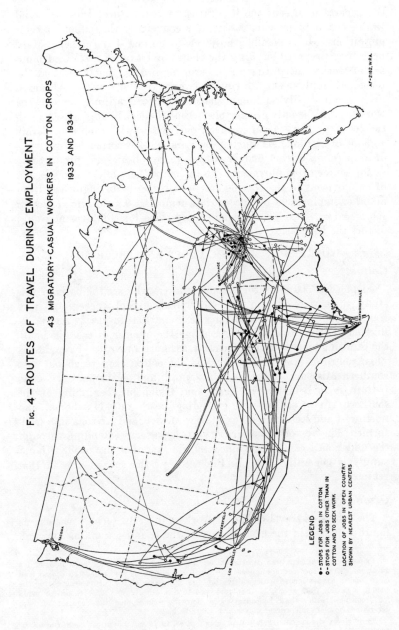

Fig. 4 – ROUTES OF TRAVEL DURING EMPLOYMENT

43 MIGRATORY-CASUAL WORKERS IN COTTON CROPS

1933 AND 1934

LEGEND

●– STOPS FOR JOBS IN COTTON
○– STOPS FOR JOBS OTHER THAN IN
COTTON AND TO SEEK WORK

LOCATION OF JOBS IN OPEN COUNTRY
SHOWN BY NEAREST URBAN CENTERS

AF-2182, W.P.A.

the general nature of the itineraries of agricultural and industrial workers, and to provide a basis for comparing the extent of their migrations. It is possible, however, to go one step further. Maps have been prepared showing the routes of travel of a selected number of workers according to the crop or process that furnished the principal employment [4] during the years 1933 and 1934. Although this is admittedly a rough means of distinguishing among the workers, it is the only practicable method that can be applied. Among the 500 migratory-casual workers, only a few with even a moderate amount of employment during 1933 and 1934 reported but one type of crop (e. g., wheat) or one process (e. g., oil and gas production) as the source of employment. In the maps that follow, the location of employment in the specific crop or process is distinguished from all other employment by appropriate symbols. The location of every job is shown, since the omission of any stops for employment would distort the itineraries.

WORKERS IN SPECIFIC CROPS AND PROCESSES [5]

Cotton.

Among the 500 migratory-casual workers who are the basis of this study, there were 43 who were clearly cotton field workers and who found enough employment during 1933 and 1934 to justify the reproduction of their itineraries. Although the number of cases is small, the resulting work patterns are clear, as figure 4 reveals. From Memphis, routes of travel of workers in the cotton crop reach out into southern Missouri, Arkansas, Mississippi, and Alabama. A second pattern is to be found in Texas and Oklahoma, beginning at the southern tip of Texas and extending north into Oklahoma, and northwest and west across Texas, New Mexico, and Arizona into California. The absence of migratory-work patterns extending through the Old South can be explained by the fact that the resident labor supply is generally equal to the needs of the cotton crop in that region.

Grain Crops.

The routes of travel of the 47 workers in grain form a pattern, as figure 5 shows, in the central part of the country, running through

---

[4] Principal employment was determined on the basis of job frequency regardless of job duration. Thus, the workers whose itineraries are shown on fig. 4 (cotton crops) had more jobs in connection with the cultivation and harvesting of the cotton crop during the combined period 1933 and 1934 than they had in any other crop. The reason for using job frequency rather than job duration is that the number, not the duration of jobs, determines how often a worker moves and where he goes.

[5] Throughout the specific crop and process figures, there is no duplication in the use of work histories. Thus, the itinerary of a worker whose principal employment was in cotton was used only once, although the itinerary may have included subsidiary jobs in grain or other crops.

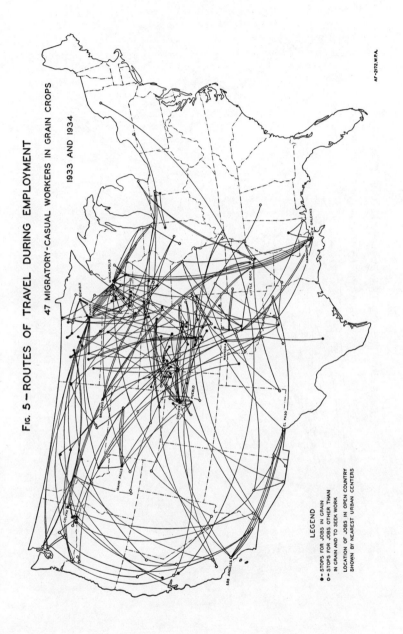

Fig. 5 – ROUTES OF TRAVEL DURING EMPLOYMENT
47 MIGRATORY-CASUAL WORKERS IN GRAIN CROPS
1933 AND 1934

LEGEND
●— STOPS FOR JOBS IN GRAIN
○— STOPS FOR JOBS OTHER THAN IN GRAIN AND TO SEEK WORK
LOCATION OF JOBS IN OPEN COUNTRY SHOWN BY NEAREST URBAN CENTERS

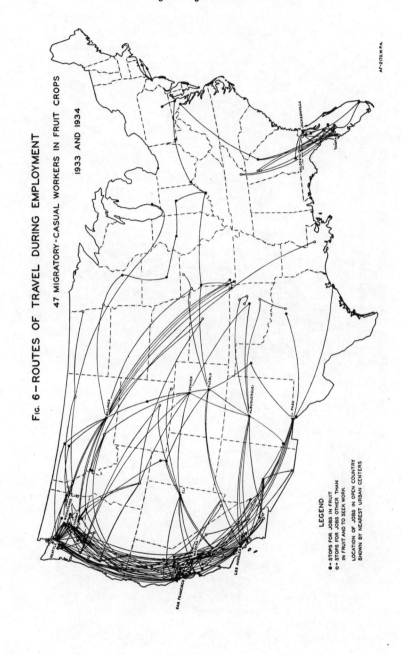

FIG. 6—ROUTES OF TRAVEL DURING EMPLOYMENT

47 MIGRATORY-CASUAL WORKERS IN FRUIT CROPS

1933 AND 1934

LEGEND

● – STOPS FOR JOBS IN FRUIT

○ – STOPS FOR JOBS OTHER THAN
    IN FRUIT AND TO SEEK WORK

LOCATION OF JOBS IN OPEN COUNTRY
SHOWN BY NEAREST URBAN CENTERS

AF-2170, W.P.A.

the "grain basket" of the double tier of States just west of the Mississippi River. From Texas north to the Canadian border, the itineraries cross and recross in Kansas, Nebraska, Iowa, Minnesota, and the Dakotas.

Fruit Crops.

Further information on the closely knit work patterns of migratory-casual laborers in agriculture is to be found in figure 6, which shows the routes of travel during employment of 47 migratory-casual workers in fruit crops. The movement of migratory-casual workers up and down the Pacific coast as they pick and pack oranges, grapefruit, peaches, prunes, apples, apricots, cherries, pears, grapes, and olives produces the best defined pattern to be found among the 500 workers studied. In the State of Washington there is an intrastate movement connecting Seattle, Wenatchee, and Yakima; a less pronounced but analogous intrastate pattern in the vicinity of San Francisco and Los Angeles is obscured by the interstate itineraries that cover the Pacific Coast States. It seems apparent from figure 6 that the three States—Washington, Oregon, and California—constitute a fairly contiguous labor market for the service of the migratory-casual worker who follows the fruit harvests.

There is evidence of a less important but definite movement of fruit workers in Florida. In the central portion of the State, the "ridge" section reaching from Tampa to Jacksonville, citrus fruit is an important winter crop. Florida is an exception to the general rule that migratory-casual workers are of little importance in the agricultural labor supply of the southern States. It is believed that further study would show that fruit and winter vegetable workers in Florida have established migratory-work patterns that are as definite, though not as numerous, as those found on the West coast.

Sugar-Beet and Berry Crops.

The sugar-beet and berry harvests provide employment for large numbers of migratory-casual workers, but the nature of the work done tends to attract migrant family groups to a greater extent than unattached workers. In both these crops the entire family can find employment within their physical capacities. Because only unattached migrants are included in this report, employment in sugar-beet and berry field work is underrepresented. Nevertheless, the itineraries presented in figure 7 are instructive. Employment in the sugar-beet fields tends to be of longer duration than the employment obtained in other crops.[6] More frequently than not, the beet worker stays through the season, roughly from May through October, and

---

[6] See fig. 24, p. 79 for duration of employment by type of crop.

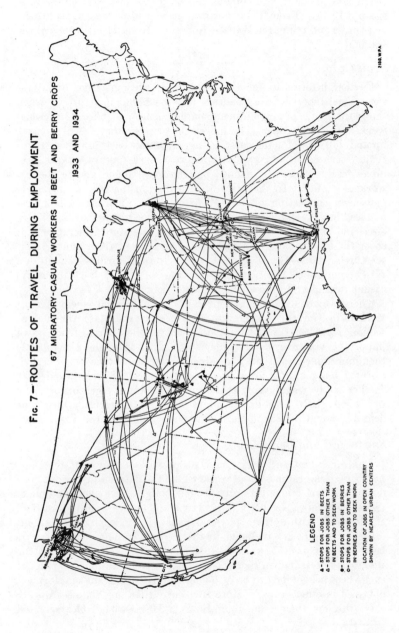

Fig. 7.—ROUTES OF TRAVEL DURING EMPLOYMENT

67 MIGRATORY-CASUAL WORKERS IN BEET AND BERRY CROPS

1933 AND 1934

LEGEND

▲– STOPS FOR JOBS IN BEETS
△– STOPS FOR JOBS OTHER THAN
    IN BEETS AND TO SEEK WORK
●– STOPS FOR JOBS IN BERRIES
○– STOPS FOR JOBS OTHER THAN
    IN BERRIES AND TO SEEK WORK

— LOCATION OF JOBS IN OPEN COUNTRY
   SHOWN BY NEAREST URBAN CENTERS

therefore has a relatively restricted extent of migration. Reference to figure 7 shows that the locations of the jobs obtained by workers in the sugar-beet fields (black triangular symbols) were confined to a small area in Minnesota and to a relatively narrow section running diagonally northwest from Colorado through parts of Nebraska and Wyoming into Montana.

The itineraries of berry field workers shown on the same map range over a wider territory, though the locations of employment have the same tendency to cluster as was found in sugar-beet employment. The berry harvest (strawberries, raspberries, etc.) is of short duration, and the worker following this crop must move rapidly to the next area if an employment sequence is to be established. Berry picking is a poorly paid and a disagreeable employment in most cases; therefore the unattached worker is likely to resort to it only when he cannot secure other types of employment.

There are two fairly well defined migratory-work patterns of berry pickers in figure 7: One runs north and south from Michigan to Louisiana with lines running into Arkansas; the other—an intra-state pattern—is confined, as far as berry field work is concerned, to the State of Washington. The routes of travel describing both of these patterns show frequent stops (open circles) for employment in other crops.

Oil and Gas.

The drilling of oil and gas wells, and the construction of pipe lines connecting the production areas with refineries and distributing centers are processes that provide the migratory-casual worker with fairly well-paid, but intermittent, employment. The unattached migratory-casual worker is by nature a "boomer", and word of a new oil field or of a large pipe-line construction job is enough to attract workers from all directions. The part that chance and rumor play in directing the workers' search for employment results in itineraries that cross and recross and present, in figure 8, a tangle of lines confined only by the limits of the more important gas and oil producing regions. These lines run from southern Texas north through Oklahoma into Kansas and east into Louisiana and Arkansas. The extreme mobility of workers in gas and oil production can be seen from movements that extend across several States without a stop for employment of any kind.

Railroad Maintenance.

Railroad maintenance in the form of extra gang work provides industrial employment for the migratory-casual worker which approaches in seasonal regularity that provided by some of the agricultural crops. As a result, the migratory-work patterns of the

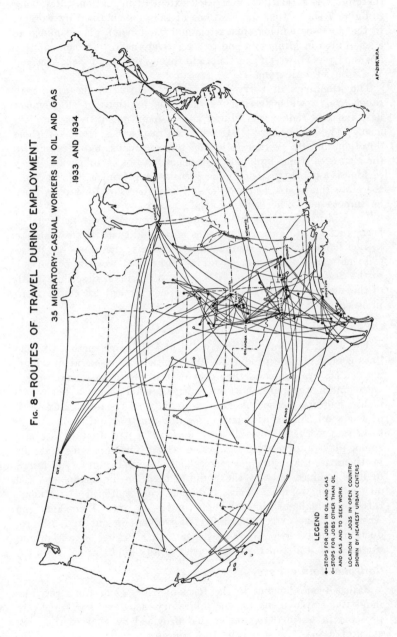

FIG. 8—ROUTES OF TRAVEL DURING EMPLOYMENT

35 MIGRATORY-CASUAL WORKERS IN OIL AND GAS

1933 AND 1934

LEGEND

●—STOPS FOR JOBS IN OIL AND GAS
○—STOPS FOR JOBS OTHER THAN OIL
     AND GAS AND TO SEEK WORK

LOCATION OF JOBS IN OPEN COUNTRY
SHOWN BY NEAREST URBAN CENTERS

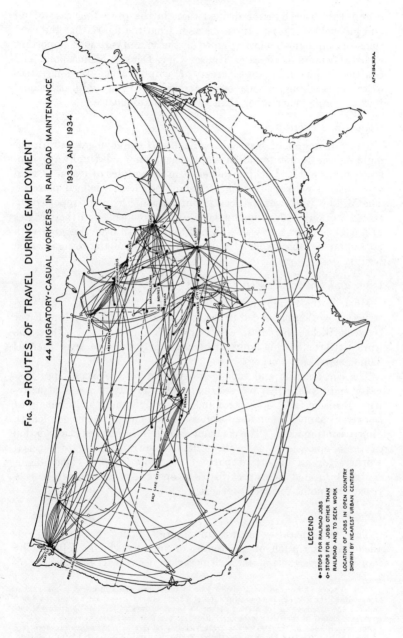

Fɪɢ. 9 – ROUTES OF TRAVEL DURING EMPLOYMENT

44 MIGRATORY-CASUAL WORKERS IN RAILROAD MAINTENANCE

1933 AND 1934

LEGEND

●— STOPS FOR RAILROAD JOBS

○— STOPS FOR JOBS OTHER THAN
    RAILROAD AND TO SEEK WORK

LOCATION OF JOBS IN OPEN COUNTRY
SHOWN BY NEAREST URBAN CENTERS

AF-2194,W.P.A.

group (fig. 9) are better defined than in the preceding case of oil and gas field workers. It can be seen from the figure that the locations of employments are grouped in the vicinity of such important railroad centers as Chicago, Kansas City, Denver, Minneapolis, and Seattle. Connecting these areas of employment are long lines of travel reaching, in some cases, across the country with occasional jobs at employment other than railroad maintenance.[7]

Road Construction.

The fair degree of seasonal regularity of employment in railroad maintenance is not found in employment on road (highway) construction projects. Lacking this element, the routes of travel of road construction workers (see fig. 10) show no clearly defined patterns. The Middle West was the location of most of the work reported by the 42 workers following this type of employment, and their routes of travel run east and west and north and south over this area with no apparent cause other than chance to explain the design which results.

Dam and Levee Construction.

Most of the employment secured by the 39 dam and levee construction workers included in the study was on the Mississippi River between Vicksburg, Miss., and Cairo, Ill. (see fig. 11). Thus, the work patterns on this figure are more nearly those of levee than of dam construction workers.

The construction and repair of levees along the Mississippi is a never ending task that has seasonal and intermittent peaks of activity. Projects for flood control and the straightening and clearing of the river channel are in operation somewhere along the river's length almost continuously. The constant shift in location and the isolation of these operations make them dependent upon migratory-casual workers for an important part of the labor supply. Memphis is centrally located in respect to these operations and therefore is a recruiting point for such workers.

Logging.

The 41 itineraries shown in figure 12 are possibly an inadequate description of the routes of travel normally followed by loggers. Nevertheless, these itineraries do reveal a tendency to-

---

[7] The absence of railroad maintenance jobs in the South and Southwest is probably to be accounted for by : (1) the plentiful supply of local labor for seasonal work in the South and (2) the extensive use of Mexican labor in the Southwest. Mexican migratory-casual workers included in the study were agricultural rather than industrial workers.

For a discussion of the Mexican migratory-casual laborer in railroad maintenance, see Taylor, Paul S., Mexican Labor in the United States, Valley of the South Platte, Colorado, University of California Publications in Economics, Berkeley, Calif., 1928, vol. VI, no. 2, pp. 62 ff.

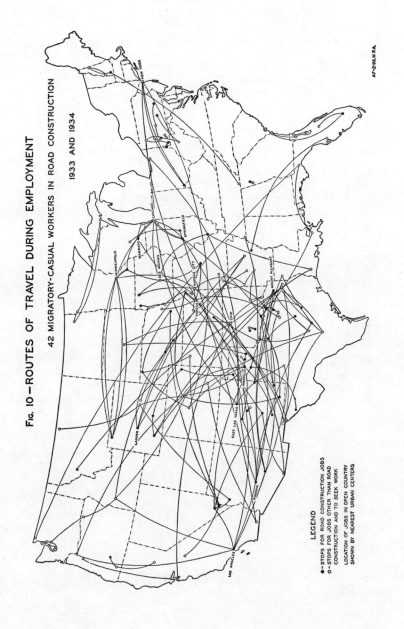

FIG. 10—ROUTES OF TRAVEL DURING EMPLOYMENT

42 MIGRATORY-CASUAL WORKERS IN ROAD CONSTRUCTION

1933 AND 1934

LEGEND

● — STOPS FOR ROAD CONSTRUCTION JOBS

○ — STOPS FOR JOBS OTHER THAN ROAD CONSTRUCTION AND TO SEEK WORK

LOCATION OF JOBS IN OPEN COUNTRY SHOWN BY NEAREST URBAN CENTERS

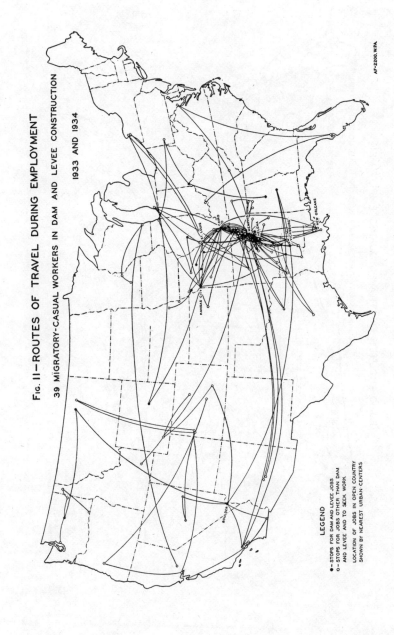

Fig. II—ROUTES OF TRAVEL DURING EMPLOYMENT

39 MIGRATORY-CASUAL WORKERS IN DAM AND LEVEE CONSTRUCTION

1933 AND 1934

LEGEND

● — STOPS FOR DAM AND LEVEE JOBS
○ — STOPS FOR JOBS OTHER THAN DAM
      AND LEVEE AND TO SEEK WORK

LOCATION OF JOBS IN OPEN COUNTRY
SHOWN BY NEAREST URBAN CENTERS

AF-2200, W.PA.

ward the distinct patterns that might be expected of workers in an industry that, depending upon weather or market conditions, is seasonal and intermittent in operation.

In two areas, western Washington and northern Minnesota, the evidence of a regular and recurring migratory-work pattern is clear. Seattle, Minneapolis, and Duluth are well-known labor markets and off-season headquarters for woodsmen, and figure 12 shows the movement from these centers into two important areas of lumbering operations.

There is also a suggestion, in figure 12, of two other and less important patterns. One is to be found in the hardwood region near Memphis, and the other in Maine, in the vicinity of Bangor. The shortage of work for woodsmen is reflected in the number of jobs other than in logging (open circles) that appear in the itineraries, particularly on the Pacific coast.[8]

In reviewing the discussion of routes of travel during employment there are several features that seem deserving of restatement in summary form. The compactness and regularity of work patterns is more pronounced among agricultural than among industrial workers. This appears to be the result more of the greater seasonal factor in agricultural employment—the regular and anticipated recurrence of work opportunities in the same area—than of any distinction in the nature of the work performed. This argument is based upon the evidence in the maps that travel patterns in agriculture were compact (fruit workers) or dispersed (berry workers), depending upon the sequence of employment that was provided within contiguous areas. Much the same result was found among industrial workers where the compact patterns for railroad maintenance and levee workers are in decided contrast to the dispersed patterns of road construction workers. Thus, seasonal recurrence and spatial sequence of employment appear to be the factors determining the extent and regularity of migration; and it is largely because these factors are more favorable in agriculture than in industry that the combined patterns of agricultural workers (see fig. 1) are more distinct and restricted in extent than are those of the industrial patterns (see figs. 2 and 3).

STATE OF PRINCIPAL EMPLOYMENT

Besides illustrating the extent of movement of migratory-casual workers and, at the same time, showing something of the work patterns that they develop, the route-of-travel maps serve the additional

---

[8] However, it would have been easy for woodsmen to get jobs other than in logging, since the slack season in logging came in midsummer when employment activity in other pursuits was at its peak. See figs. 25 and 26.

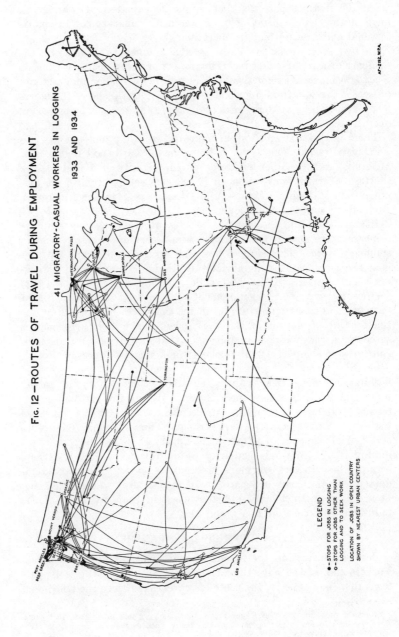

Fig. 12—ROUTES OF TRAVEL DURING EMPLOYMENT

41 MIGRATORY-CASUAL WORKERS IN LOGGING

1933 AND 1934

LEGEND

● — STOPS FOR JOBS IN LOGGING
○ — STOPS FOR JOBS OTHER THAN
      LOGGING AND TO SEEK WORK

LOCATION OF JOBS IN OPEN COUNTRY
SHOWN BY NEAREST URBAN CENTERS

function of indicating the relative importance of the several States as sources of employment opportunities. However, the fact that all employments during migration are recorded on the maps without any indication of their duration may fail to distinguish properly the relative importance of the States in terms of maximum employment obtained.

In order to bring out clearly their importance as sources of employment, the States in which the maximum amount of employment [9] was secured in each of the 2 years, 1933 and 1934, have been determined, and are presented in figures 13 to 16 and in appendix table 2. A summary of the detailed data of appendix table 2 is presented in table 3 below. This summary table adds to the information presented earlier on the relative extent of migration among the three types of workers.

TABLE 3.—NUMBER OF STATES DESIGNATED AS PLACE OF PRINCIPAL EMPLOYMENT, AND PROPORTION OF WORKERS INCLUDED IN THE 5 STATES MOST FREQUENTLY DESIGNATED, 500 MIGRATORY-CASUAL WORKERS, 1933–34

Type of worker	Number of States designated		Proportion of workers in 5 States most frequently designated	
	1933	1934	1933	1934
	Number	*Number*	*Percent*	*Percent*
Total	43	39	40	41
Agricultural	26	27	52	52
Industrial	29	32	46	41
Combination [1]	40	36	29	31

[1] Workers combining agricultural and industrial employment.

A smaller number of States was designated as the location of principal employment for agricultural than for industrial or for combination workers, and over one-half of the agricultural workers were included in the five most important States. Among industrial workers the location of principal employment included more States, and there was a smaller proportion of workers included in the five States most frequently designated. Workers following combination employment found their principal employment in the greatest number of States, and had the smallest proportion of workers included in the five States of most importance.

It should be noted that three States—California, Washington, and Texas—are included among the first five States for the total and for each of the three types of workers. The fourth and fifth States were Minnesota and Arkansas for the total and for agricultural

[9] The duration of all jobs in one State, regardless of sequence, for workers of each of the three types was combined for 1933 and 1934 in determining the maximum of employment.

workers, Minnesota and Missouri for industrial workers, and Kansas and Arkansas for combination workers. The report by States may be found in appendix table 2, and a graphic representation of the information appears in figures 13 to 16.

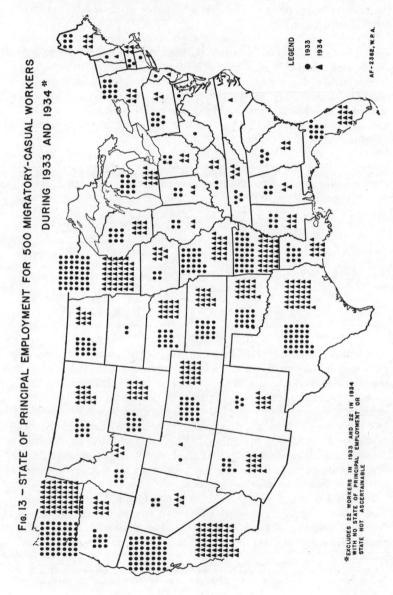

Fig. 13 – STATE OF PRINCIPAL EMPLOYMENT FOR 500 MIGRATORY-CASUAL WORKERS DURING 1933 AND 1934*

LEGEND ● 1933 ▲ 1934

AF-2362, W.P.A.

*EXCLUDES 22 WORKERS IN 1933 AND 22 IN 1934 WITH NO STATE OF PRINCIPAL EMPLOYMENT OR STATE NOT ASCERTAINABLE

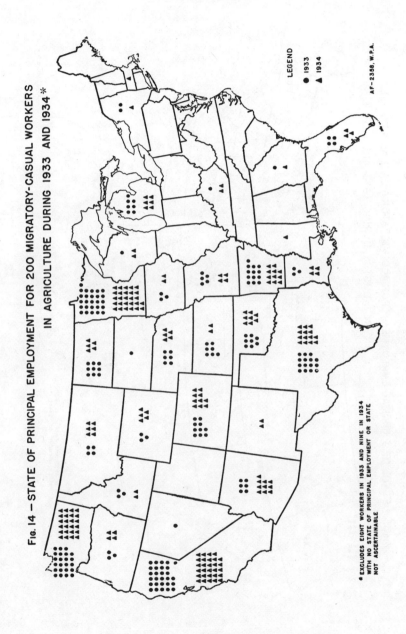

FIG. 14 — STATE OF PRINCIPAL EMPLOYMENT FOR 200 MIGRATORY-CASUAL WORKERS IN AGRICULTURE DURING 1933 AND 1934 *

LEGEND
● 1933
▲ 1934

AF-2388, W.P.A.

* EXCLUDES EIGHT WORKERS IN 1933 AND NINE IN 1934 WITH NO STATE OF PRINCIPAL EMPLOYMENT OR STATE NOT ASCERTAINABLE

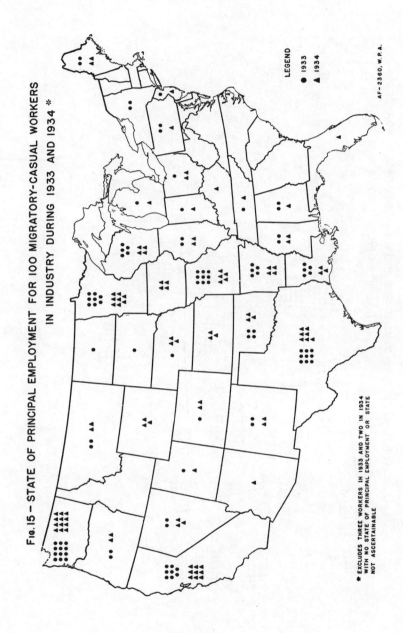

Fig. 15 — STATE OF PRINCIPAL EMPLOYMENT FOR 100 MIGRATORY-CASUAL WORKERS IN INDUSTRY DURING 1933 AND 1934 *

LEGEND
● 1933
▲ 1934

AF—2360, W.P.A.

* EXCLUDES THREE WORKERS IN 1933 AND TWO IN 1934 WITH NO STATE OF PRINCIPAL EMPLOYMENT OR STATE NOT ASCERTAINABLE

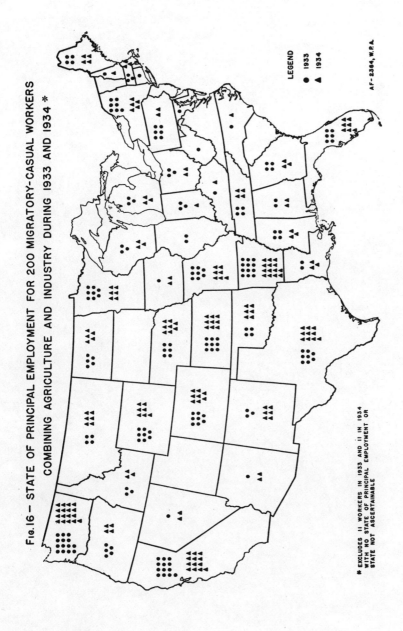

FIG. 16 — STATE OF PRINCIPAL EMPLOYMENT FOR 200 MIGRATORY-CASUAL WORKERS COMBINING AGRICULTURE AND INDUSTRY DURING 1933 AND 1934 *

LEGEND
● 1933
▲ 1934

AF-2364, W.P.A.

* EXCLUDES 11 WORKERS IN 1933 AND 11 IN 1934 WITH NO STATE OF PRINCIPAL EMPLOYMENT OR STATE NOT ASCERTAINABLE

Chapter III

THE CHARACTERISTICS OF MIGRATORY-CASUAL EMPLOYMENT

ECAUSE THIS STUDY of migratory-casual workers was made during the depression years 1933 and 1934, it is to be expected that the characteristics of jobs held during these years would differ in some degree from those that might have been observed under more satisfactory employment conditions. An appraisal of this divergence, and of the probable extent to which the data for 1933 and 1934 would deviate from those of "normal" times, must of necessity be left for further study. Meanwhile, the data obtained in this investigation reveal several characteristics of migratory-casual work that are basic, and would persist through both boom and depression. As pointed out in chapter I, these essential characteristics are: (1) shortness of job duration, necessitating that each worker secure a number of jobs in order to earn each year sufficient income for subsistence; (2) seasonality of work, permitting the worker to devise a rough yearly schedule of jobs which may be repeated year after year; and (3) wide geographical separation of work, requiring migration from one job to another. The last of these characteristics has already been dealt with in chapter II; the first two—duration and number of jobs, and seasonality of employment—are the subjects for discussion in this chapter.

DURATION OF JOBS

For the 500 workers included in this study, the average duration of jobs [1] was about 2 months (including holidays and time lost during employment) in both 1933 and 1934 (see fig. 17). As reported by the workers, more jobs lasted 1 to 2 months than any other time interval, and about one-half of all jobs lasted from 1 to 3 months. As may be observed from table 4 only a small proportion of the

---

[1] For the purpose of this study a "job" was defined as a continuous employment in one district at one pursuit, regardless of the number of employers involved and regardless of time lost on the job because of holidays and lay-offs. A harvest hand, for example, may have helped with the harvest at a number of neighboring farms, and yet have been considered to have had only one job, provided the other conditions were fulfilled. It should be borne in mind that the data on duration of jobs are given in terms of total jobs, rather than in terms of workers. The bases of table 4 are thus 1,190 and 1,107 *jobs*, rather than 500 *workers*.

jobs lasted a very short, or a relatively long, period of time; in 1933 only 6 percent, and in 1934 only 8 percent of all jobs lasted less than 8 days, and the same or a smaller proportion of them lasted longer than 6 months.

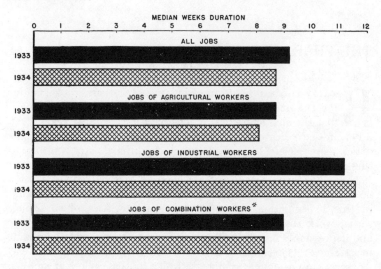

Fig. 17 — AVERAGE DURATION OF JOBS HELD BY 500
MIGRATORY — CASUAL WORKERS
1933 — 1934

*Workers combining agricultural
and industrial employment   AF — 2336, W. P. A.

The duration of the jobs held by the three groups of workers— agricultural, industrial, and combination—was not uniform. Jobs in agriculture were consistently shortest; jobs in industry lasted longest; and the average duration of jobs of workers who combined agricultural with industrial employment was intermediate between these extremes. These differences are to be expected. As will be explained in chapter IV, the agricultural workers were employed largely in such short-time seasonal jobs as harvesting; the industrial workers were most often engaged in logging, construction, or other work in which the jobs held are naturally of longer duration; and the third group of workers held in about equal proportions the shorter jobs of agriculture and the longer jobs of industry.

Not only did migratory-casual workers in industry hold the longest jobs, but these jobs were also slightly longer in 1934 than in 1933 (see fig. 17). In contrast, the average length of the jobs held by the other two groups of workers decreased in 1934. The net result of the changes among the three groups of workers was a decrease in the average duration of all jobs in 1934 compared with the average duration in the preceding year.

TABLE 4.—DURATION OF JOBS HELD BY 500 MIGRATORY-CASUAL WORKERS, 1933-34

Duration of jobs	1933				1934			
	Total	Jobs of agricultural workers	Jobs of industrial workers	Jobs of combination workers[1]	Total	Jobs of agricultural workers	Jobs of industrial workers	Jobs of combination workers[1]
All jobs	[2] 1,190	486	228	476	[3] 1,107	471	205	431
	Percent distribution							
All jobs	100	100	100	100	100	100	100	100
Less than 8 days	6	6	8	5	8	11	5	6
8 to 15 days	6	6	6	6	8	9	7	8
15 to 30 days	5	4	3	6	7	7	4	8
1 to 2 months	30	34	22	32	27	27	18	30
2 to 3 months	20	23	19	19	20	20	23	19
3 to 4 months	16	13	16	18	13	11	20	12
4 to 6 months	11	10	18	8	12	12	14	11
6 months and more	6	4	8	6	5	3	9	6
Median duration of jobs held in weeks [4]	9.2	8.7	11.2	9.0	8.7	8.1	11.6	8.3

[1] Jobs of workers combining agricultural and industrial employment.
[2] Includes 16 jobs whose duration was not ascertainable, but which were distributed pro rata, and excludes 29 jobs obtained in the off-season.
[3] Excludes 35 jobs obtained in the off-season.
[4] Medians computed for months and converted to weeks on the basis of 4.33 weeks per month. Computed duration of jobs includes holidays and time lost on jobs.

Among the variations in the duration of migratory-casual jobs, those related to the three different types of work are much more striking than those which result from a comparison of 1934 with 1933. Although there was a general decrease in the duration of jobs from 1933 to 1934, the change was not enough to obscure a decided similarity of employment duration in the 2 years. This similarity is one indication of the tendency, to be further illustrated later, for the employment characteristics of individual years to resemble one another, regardless of how wide the range of variable elements may be within any single year.

NUMBER OF JOBS

The significance of the fact that the average duration of the jobs held in 1933 and 1934 was about 2 months becomes clear in the light of information on the number of jobs held during each year. Few of the 500 migratory-casual workers had anything approaching full employment, and most of them held only 1, 2, or 3 jobs each year.[2] Less than one-fifth of the workers held more than three jobs in each of the 2 years, and less than one-tenth of them had more than four jobs during each year (see table 5).

TABLE 5.—NUMBER OF JOBS HELD BY 500 MIGRATORY-CASUAL WORKERS, 1933–34

Number of jobs	1933				1934			
	Total	Type of worker			Total	Type of worker		
		Agricultural	Industrial	Combination [1]		Agricultural	Industrial	Combination [1]
All workers [2]	500	200	100	200	500	200	100	200
	Percent distribution							
All workers	100	100	100	100	100	100	100	100
No job	4	4	3	5	5	4	3	5
1 job	24	28	26	20	27	29	26	26
2 jobs	31	27	36	34	34	30	45	34
3 jobs	23	22	20	25	19	16	20	23
4 jobs	9	9	8	9	9	13	5	7
5 jobs	5	6	5	4	4	5		3
6 jobs	2	2	1	2	1	1		1
7 jobs	1	1	1	1	1	1		1
8 jobs								
9 jobs	1	1			(3)	1	1	
Median number of jobs per worker	2.7	2.7	2.6	2.8	2.5	2.6	2.5	2.6

[1] Workers combining agricultural and industrial employment.
[2] Excludes 29 jobs obtained in the off-season in 1933, and 35 jobs obtained in the off-season in 1934.
[3] Less than 0.5 percent.

The absence of any considerable portion of workers with four or more jobs suggests that the depression has had some effect upon the high labor turnover which in times past has been one of the characteristics of migratory-casual employment, especially in such industrial pursuits as tunnel work, logging, and road construction. High labor turnover, as it existed in migratory-casual work before the depression, was a direct result of the failure of legitimate protests to correct employment abuses. Faced with low pay and working conditions sometimes fantastically bad, and denied the right or the opportunity of labor organization, the workers developed the habit of working only long enough on one job to get a stake and then going off the job until the stake was spent. Such a practice was partially dependent upon the probability of securing work

---

[2] The proportion of migratory-casual workers that failed altogether to secure work in 1933 and 1934 cannot be determined here, since this study is confined to workers who had some work in one year or the other. Thus, all those shown in table 5 as having had no work during one of the years had work during the other. It should not be inferred from the smallness of the proportion of workers in this study who had no jobs that migratory-casual workers in general were so fortunate in finding employment in 1933 and 1934. The present study does not include workers who had been unemployed since the beginning of 1933 for the obvious reason that such workers could contribute nothing to a study of employment patterns during migration.

whenever the stake was exhausted, a condition which practically vanished during the depression.[3]

A comparison of the frequency of jobs per worker in the 2 years shows that in 1934 there was an increase in the proportion of workers with only one and two jobs. Yet, as with the variation between the years in the duration of jobs, the amount of the change was not great. According to table 5, the median number of jobs per worker changed but little from 1933 to 1934, and once again the consistency of the results for the 2 years is worthy of note. Basically, the work patterns of migratory-casual workers are time-patterns in which the variations within the year are clearly recurrent. The explanation of this fact is to be found in an examination of the relationship between employment and the progression of the seasons.

SEASONALITY OF EMPLOYMENT

A demand for the labor of migratory-casual workers exists in some degree throughout the entire year; in each month of both 1933 and 1934 some of the 500 workers had been at work. But, as is well known, migratory-casual workers are much more active at one season than at another. The extent to which the peak months provide more employment than do other months may be observed in figure 18, which shows the number of man-weeks worked by the 500 workers during each month of 1933 and 1934. At the low point in the seasonal decline of activity, reached early in the winter, the 500 workers reported less than 600 man-weeks of employment per month. But at the top of the summertime peak, reached in July, activity had more than doubled, and the workers reported approximately 1,200 man-weeks per month. However, during this midsummer peak the workers fell far short of full-time employment.

The consistency of the relationship between migratory-casual employment and the seasons of the year can be seen by a comparison of the curve of activity for 1933 with that of 1934 (see fig. 18). It will be observed that the line which represents the activity during each month of 1934 repeats the essential characteristics of the line for

---

[3] The notorius "three-gang system"—one gang leaving, one gang working, and one gang arriving on the job—characterized much migratory-casual work prior to the depression. Probably the most remarkable record of labor turnover on a migratory-casual job was reported by Rev. Oscar H. McGill in the Hearings Before the Commission on Industrial Relations. According to Reverend McGill the labor force employed in building the Milwaukee tunnel through the mountains east of Seattle changed completely on an average of every 5 days. Thus, out of 1,000 workers employed, 200 arrived and departed every day. See Report of Commission on Industrial Relations, S. Doc. No. 415, 64th Cong., Washington, D. C., 1916, vol. V, p. 4384.

See also Howd, Cloice R., Industrial Relations in the West Coast Lumber Industry, U. S. Department of Labor, Bureau of Labor Statistics, Bulletin 349, p. 38. Howd estimated that the labor turnover in the logging camps in the Pacific Northwest in 1921 was considerably more than 500 percent per year.

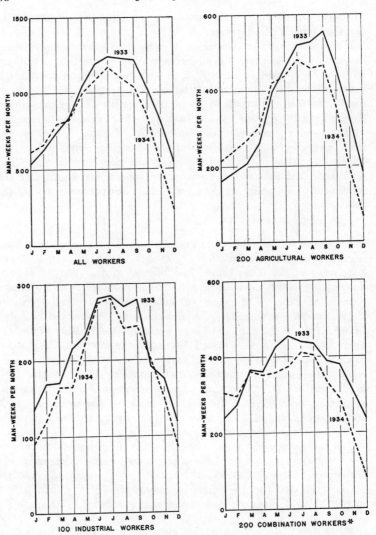

Fɪɢ. 18 — SEASONAL FLUCTUATION IN THE ACTIVITY OF
500 MIGRATORY - CASUAL WORKERS
1933 – 1934

* Workers, combining agricultural
and industrial employment

AF – 2372 W. P. A.

1933.[4] In both years there was a progressive rise in activity from January to July, and in both there was a continual decline after July. The nature of the late summer and autumn decline is the same during each year; after July the curve falls off only slightly until September, but from this point on, it falls off steeply until the December trough is reached.

The progression of the seasons affected the various types of migratory-casual workers in somewhat different ways, yet the 1933 peculiarities of each group tended, like the variations for the 500 workers as a group, to be duplicated in 1934. As shown in figure 18, the monthly variation in activity among the workers in agriculture generally resembled that of all workers considered together except for (1) a later maturing peak season in 1933, which came in September; and (2) a more complete cessation of activity in the winter, especially in December 1934.

The curve in figure 18 representing the workers in industry shows that seasonality had much the same effect upon these workers as it had upon those engaged only in agriculture. Both the increase in their activities from January to June, and the decline from September to December are as sharp as that noted for the agricultural workers, and the wintertime slack period is equally inactive in comparison with the peak season. Again, there is close agreement between the monthly variations of 1933 and 1934.

Workers who followed a combination of agricultural and industrial jobs experienced the least seasonal fluctuation in employment. The curves showing their activity by months lack the pronounced midsummer peak that is found in the curves for the other two groups (see fig. 18); they secured more employment in the winter and spring, but decidedly less in the summer and fall. From April on, workers in this group found distinctly less employment in 1934 than in the preceding year.

Month of Obtaining Jobs.

In view of the relationship between the progression of the seasons and the activity of migratory-casual workers, it is evident that more jobs were obtained in certain months of each year than in

---

[4] Although the general shape of the two curves is the same, the curve for 1934 falls off more sharply in the latter part of the year than the curve for 1933. This difference in the 2 curves represents a partial collapse, toward the end of 1934, in the activity of the 500 workers. It appears to be associated with the fact that the 500 workers studied were uniformly affected by adverse conditions during the summer and fall of 1934, since all of them obtained assistance from transient bureaus at some time during the first 6 months of 1935. Thus, the decline shown in fig. 18 does not necessarily mean a general decline in the activity of all migratory-casual workers, both on and off relief, during these months. For this reason 1933 is probably more nearly representative of general conditions of migratory-casual employment during the depression than is 1934.

others. The close relationship between the month and the workers' success in finding employment may be seen in figure 19, which compares the monthly fluctuations in new jobs obtained in 1933 and 1934. Despite the greater decline in jobs during November and December 1934,[5] the general agreement of the 2 years is close, both for the 500 workers considered as a group, and for the workers in each of the 3 component classifications.

Fluctuations in the number of new jobs are governed by the fluctuations in seasonal activity described earlier. The curves showing monthly activity in terms of man-weeks of employment and the curves showing the number of new jobs obtained each month are not, however, identical. This is the result of a third factor, namely, the duration of jobs, which also varies according to the season of the year. Since the peak of the year's activity in migratory-casual work comes in the summer, the jobs obtained earlier in the year tend to last through the months of peak activity, and those obtained later naturally are of shorter duration. The exact effect of the season in which a job was obtained upon the duration of jobs may be seen in the comparison of the median duration of the jobs obtained at the four different seasons as shown in figure 20. It may also be observed from this figure that the seasonal variation in the duration of jobs, like the other characteristics of migratory-casual employment, was repeated with little change in each of the 2 years.

LENGTH OF MIGRATORY PERIOD AND OFF-SEASON

It is a common practice for many migratory-casual workers to spend part of each year on the road, working or seeking work, and then to withdraw from the labor market during the period when the chances of finding work are small. For workers following this practice, the year is divided into two complementary periods: the migratory period, which they spend in working or seeking work; and the off-season, which they spend in waiting until the advancement of the season revives employment opportunities.[6] Since these two periods are adjusted to fit the yearly rise and fall in the demand for migratory-casual labor, the off-season ordinarily comes in the winter, and the migratory period usually covers the spring, summer, and fall.

---

[5] See footnote 4, p. 59.

[6] During the interview each worker was asked whether he followed this custom. Those replying in the affirmative were asked to designate the duration of the migratory and the off-season periods for the 2 years 1933–34. For examples of workers with regular migratory and off-season periods, see the personal histories of Jesús Lopez and John Peterson, pp. 95–97, ch. V.

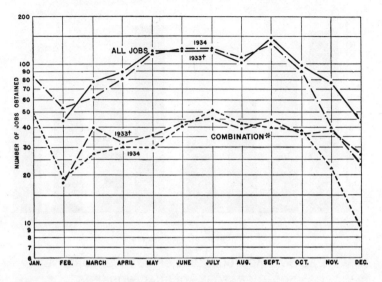

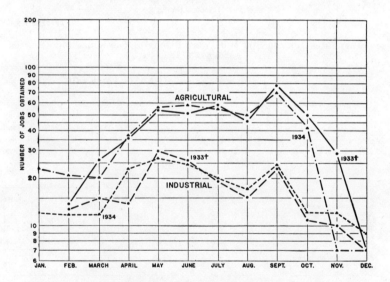

FIG. 19 — MONTHS OF OBTAINING JOBS IN 1933 AND 1934
500 MIGRATORY-CASUAL WORKERS

✻ Workers combining agricultural
and industrial employment

† Number of jobs obtained in January 1933
not ascertainable

AF-2332, W. P. A.

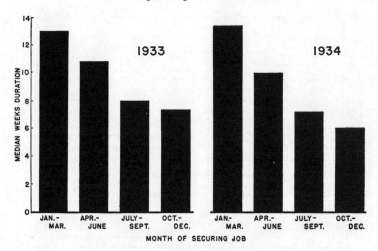

Fɪɢ. 20-AVERAGE DURATION OF JOBS SECURED BY
500 MIGRATORY-CASUAL WORKERS,
1933-1934

AF-2356, W.P.A.

Tᴀʙʟᴇ 6.—Dᴜʀᴀᴛɪᴏɴ ᴏғ Mɪɢʀᴀᴛᴏʀʏ Pᴇʀɪᴏᴅ ᴏғ 500 Mɪɢʀᴀᴛᴏʀʏ-Cᴀsᴜᴀʟ
Wᴏʀᴋᴇʀs, 1933–34

Duration of migratory period	Total		Type of worker					
			Agricultural		Industrial		Combination [1]	
	1933	1934	1933	1934	1933	1934	1933	1934
All workers	500	500	200	200	100	100	200	200
	Percent distribution							
All workers	100	100	100	100	100	100	100	100
No migratory period	3	4	3	3	--------	--------	5	5
Less than 25 weeks	3	2	5	4	1	--------	1	1
25 to 32 weeks	15	15	16	17	13	15	14	14
33 to 40 weeks	30	30	33	34	32	32	26	25
41 to 48 weeks	8	7	8	7	9	9	8	6
49 to 52 weeks	41	42	35	35	45	44	46	49
Median duration of migratory period in weeks	41	41	39	39	45	44	45	48

[1] Workers combining agricultural and industrial employment.

This does not mean that all workers follow a rigid scheme for
apportioning their time within the year. About two-fifths of the
workers in this study, for example, had practically no off-season during either 1933 or 1934 (see table 6). However, a majority of the
workers regularly remained on the road less than the full year; and

the median length of the migratory period for the 500 workers was 41 weeks in each year (see fig. 21).

Because each of the three types of migratory-casual employment has its own peculiar seasonal variations, the length of the migratory period for each type of worker varied considerably from the average for all workers. The shortest average migratory period was that of workers in agriculture, who spent about 39 weeks working or seeking work. This period was exceeded by that of workers in industry, whose migratory period averaged 45 weeks. The longest period was that of workers following a combination of employment in agriculture and industry, whose migratory period in 1934 was 48 weeks (see fig. 21).

The length of time represented by the off-season varied, of course, with the length of the migratory period. Thus, workers in agriculture had on the average the longest off-season, a period of 13 weeks each year; workers in industry had the next longest, with 7 weeks in 1933 and 8 weeks in 1934; and workers in the third group had the shortest off-season, with 7 weeks in 1933 and only 4 weeks in 1934. Some of the workers had no regular off-season during either of the years. Excluding them, the off-season most frequently reported lasted from 12 to 20 weeks (see appendix table 4).

During the off-season these workers were almost wholly unemployed. A few of them picked up odd jobs, but the total off-season employment was small. Throughout the 2-year period, the 500 workers secured only 64 jobs during the off-season; whereas, they secured 2,297 jobs during the migratory periods of the 2 years (see table 4).

EMPLOYMENT AND UNEMPLOYMENT DURING THE MIGRATORY PERIOD

Assuming that a satisfactory year for migratory-casual workers is one in which employment would cover the greater part of the migratory period, then the years 1933 and 1934 were decidedly unsuccessful years for the 500 workers included in this study. After losing an average of about 3 months each year in the off-season, many workers were also unemployed through a large part of the migratory period. Some indication of the extent of idleness during the migratory period was given when it was pointed out in the discussion of the number and duration of migratory-casual jobs, for example, that most of the workers held only one, two, or three jobs each year, and that the average duration of each of those jobs was about 2 months. In addition, it was shown that among the 500 workers, the busiest month of either year, July 1933 (see fig. 18), supplied only 1,250 man-weeks of employment out of approximately 2,160 man-

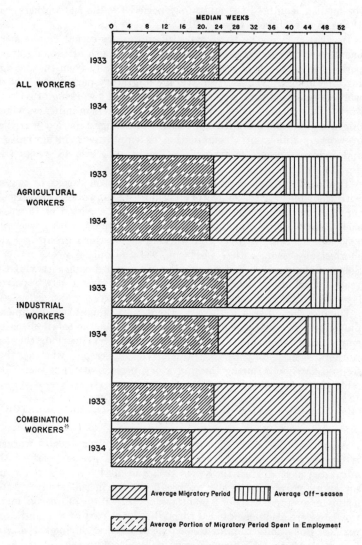

MEDIAN WEEKS

ALL WORKERS
1933
1934

AGRICULTURAL
WORKERS
1933
1934

INDUSTRIAL
WORKERS
1933
1934

COMBINATION
WORKERS*
1933
1934

///// Average Migratory Period ||||| Average Off-season

///// Average Portion of Migratory Period Spent in Employment

FIG. 21– AVERAGE MIGRATORY, EMPLOYMENT,
AND OFF–SEASON PERIODS
500 MIGRATORY–CASUAL WORKERS
1933–1934

*Workers combining Agricultural
and Industrial Employment.

AF-2342, W.P.A.

weeks possible.[7]   More specifically, a distribution of the time spent
in employment by the 500 workers shows that the median period was
24 weeks in 1933 and 21 weeks in 1934 (see appendix table 5).   Thus,
as may be observed in figure 21, in 1933 nearly one-half—and in 1934
exactly one-half—of the migratory period of all workers was spent
without employment.   In none of the three groups during either year
did the amount of time employed equal as much as three-fifths of the
migratory period and among workers following a combination of
agricultural and industrial employments during 1934, the productive
portion of the year comprised only 37 percent of the entire migratory
period.

It is not known precisely how the proportion of time lost during
migration in depression years compares with that lost by migratory-
casual workers in less stringent periods, since comparable data for
earlier years are not available.   Although it seems evident that the
amount of unemployment during migration in 1933 and 1934 was
greater than in normal times, there is little doubt that the unpro-
ductive part of the migratory period is large at any time.   Necessarily, the migratory-casual worker wastes much time and motion
because of the lack of proper direction into the nearest and timeliest
field for labor.   Even for seasonal work in which the date of the
opening of jobs is known in advance, the worker often arrives at the
job too late or too soon.   He may be unaware of a labor shortage in
a nearby community, or he may migrate in response to a rumor of a
labor shortage only to find that the rumor had been spread so far that
an oversupply of workers had arrived before him.   In addition to
the regular slack winter season there are a number of periods between
jobs when, whether they wish it or not, workers are idle while waiting
for new jobs to begin.   Thus, the migratory-casual worker is faced
not only with the imperfect adjustment of the supply of labor to
the demand, but also with the difficulties resulting from the lack of
direction of the workers.

During the depression this situation became acute.   Even an
efficient method of controlling the flow of labor in accordance with
demand, which would solve many of the difficulties of normal times,
would be of little use during a period when the oversupply of labor
amounts to a glut in the market.[8]   With more workers than jobs

---

[7] An estimate for comparative purposes arrived at by multiplying 500 workers by
4.33 weeks.

[8] Of course there were some exceptions.   How the lack of proper information among
migratory-casual workers may result in a labor shortage during a time of widespread
unemployment is illustrated by the fact of a shortage of apple harvesters in some parts
of the Wenatchee and Yakima Valleys, Wash., in the fall of 1935.   This district had
experienced such a large oversupply of workers during the apple-picking seasons of 1933
and 1934 that great numbers of workers failed to return in 1935, and a serious and costly
labor shortage resulted.

at all times, the market for migratory-casual labor is further crowded by migrants newly recruited from the general pool of unemployed. With the jobs normally filled by migratory-casual workers being preempted by the "homeguard", and with many of the industries which would ordinarily supply jobs suspended by the depression, the probability of finding work in areas of usual employment is greatly reduced.

Despite this increased scarcity of jobs, the workers included in this report do not appear to have curtailed their migrations in search of work. According to the averages shown in figure 21, a decrease in time spent in employment is most often accompanied either by little change in the average time spent in migration, or else—as in the case of the combination workers in 1934—by an appreciable increase.[9] It is easy to see why this was true. One of the unique characteristics of migratory-casual work is the extreme flexibility of the labor demand at peak seasons. However acute the oversupply of labor, the possibilities of obtaining *some* work are always present. Many of the crops and processes using migratory-casual labor— especially the agricultural pursuits—can absorb an extremely large number of workers for a very short time at the height of their season, and at such times an oversupply of labor (from the employer's point of view) is difficult to imagine. Moreover, the nature of migratory-casual employment is such that the sharing of jobs among all workers is an automatic and inevitable process. The worker ordinarily secures a number of jobs each year, all of them of short duration. The chief requirements for obtaining a job are merely that the worker be on hand, and have no obvious handicaps. If there are more workers than jobs, a person who has failed to secure one job stands an equal chance to secure the next, and the probability of continual failure throughout the migratory period is thereby reduced. These are the characteristics of migratory-casual labor that make it appealing to so many unemployed persons. The fact that there is ordinarily, even under the most stringent conditions, some work to be obtained obscures the inadequacy of that work.[10]

---

[9] It is altogether possible that the average time spent in migration had changed little during the depression. The amount of time spent by the workers studied does not appear to be in disagreement with that observed of other migratory-casual workers during other periods. See for example, Hathway, Marion, The Migratory Worker and Family Life, University of Chicago Press, Chicago, 1934, pp. 84–89.

[10] Some notion of the unique nature of the seasonal demand in some of the crops employing migratory-casual workers may be obtained from a recent study of farm labor in the Yakima Valley, Wash. According to this study, "More hired labor was employed [in hop picking] during the second week of September than during any other week of the year. It amounted to about 200,000 days of labor. Only about 29,000 days of labor were required during the next to [the] last week in August, when pear picking was at its height; about 66,000 days of labor [per week] were required when apple picking was at its height; and an average of around 3,000 days were required for each of the last 8 weeks

YEARLY EARNINGS

In exchange for his labor the migratory-casual worker obtains a meager income at best. His low yearly earnings are a direct result of factors that were given a prominent place in the general discussion of the migratory-casual worker in chapter I. Short-time jobs, seasonal and intermittent employment, work that is principally unskilled and semiskilled, an overcrowded labor market—all these are conditions that make migratory-casual workers one of the most exploited groups in the total labor supply. To say that workers are exploited is, of course, to pass a judgment on the wages that they receive. Factual support for this judgment is to be found in a tabulation of the yearly net earnings of the 500 migratory-casual workers included in the study (see appendix table 6 and fig. 22).

The earnings data shown in appendix table 6 represent the net cash income received during each of the 2 years, 1933 and 1934. The meaning of net cash income requires some explanation. The yearly earnings of the 500 workers were reported on the field schedules of this study as gross or net income, depending upon the way in which the worker could report his earnings more precisely. Gross income was defined as the total earnings computed in dollars before deductions were made by employers for housing, meals, transportation, and similar charges; and net income was the total cash wage actually received after these deductions had been made.[11] The money equivalent of the goods or services received by a considerable number of the migratory-casual workers in addition to their cash wages could be determined only by resort to a highly arbitrary procedure based upon the assumption that these perquisites were uniform in number and value. It was decided, therefore, to convert gross earnings into net earnings.[12] Although this procedure was only slightly less arbitrary than that mentioned above, it had the distinct advantage of being more immediately based upon data derived from interviews with the workers.

In making the conversion, it was found that the difference between gross and net earnings was greatest for agricultural workers and

---

of the calendar year 1935, when there was only dairying and general farm work to do."
See Landis, Paul H., and Brooks, Melvin S., Farm Labor in the Yakima Valley, Wash., Rural Sociology Series in Farm Labor, no. 1, Washington State College, Pullman, Wash., 1936.

[11] Nearly one-half of the 500 workers reported that deductions were made from their earnings by employers for some of the services supplied.

[12] This was done by dividing each of the three types of workers—agricultural, industrial, and combination—according to whether they reported yearly income as net or gross. Statistical frequency distributions were made of net and gross earnings separately, and a conversion factor was derived which could be used to convert gross to net earnings. Statistically, there was sufficient evidence of consistency in these distributions for the 2 years to justify this process.

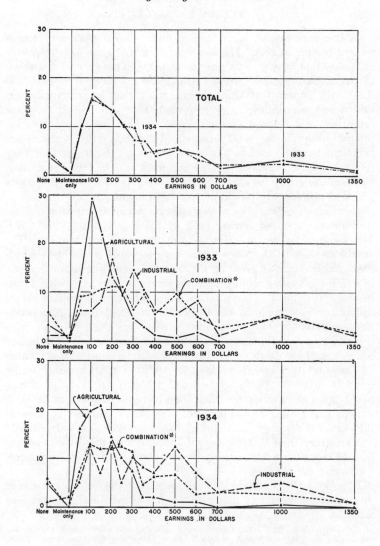

FIG. 22 – NET YEARLY EARNINGS OF 500
MIGRATORY-CASUAL WORKERS
1933-1934

* Workers combining agricultural
and industrial employment

AF – 2368, W.P.A.

least for workers at a combination of agricultural and industrial pursuits. The effect of converting gross to net earnings was to reduce somewhat the yearly earnings of each of the three groups of workers; [13] but since conversions were necessary for only about one-half of the workers, the effect on the total was to accentuate the smallness of the earnings without invalidating them for use as a *general indication* of the range and average amount of income.

Several striking facts are found in appendix table 6. Yearly earnings for the entire group ranged from maintenance to approximately $1,350 a year, but the most frequent earnings were between maintenance and $250 a year. According to table 7, the agricultural worker had the lowest median earning ($110 to $124), so low, in fact, that even the knowledge that he was likely to receive a larger part of his earnings in the form of perquisites does not account for his low earning status in comparison with workers in the other two groups.[14] Industrial workers had the widest spread between low and high yearly earnings, but net incomes of over $500 a year were few in number and the median earnings were $257 in 1933 and $272 in 1934. The yearly earnings of workers following a combination of agricultural and industrial employments occupy an intermediate position between the low of agriculture and the high of industry. The median earnings of this group were $223 in 1933 and $203 in 1934. The range and the concentration of individual earnings for each of the three groups are shown in figure 22.

Before attempting a conclusion on the relative earnings of migratory-casual workers in agriculture, industry, and a combination of the two, it is necessary to take into account the amount of employment obtained during the year. Earlier in this chapter the median duration of employment during migration was shown. When this information is brought into comparison with median earnings, a basis is provided for a conclusion as to relative yearly earnings.

---

[13] Had the conversions been to gross instead of net, the median earnings for agricultural workers would have been approximately $200 in both 1933 and 1934; for industrial workers, approximately $400 in both years; and for combination workers the median would have been approximately $275 in 1933 and $220 in 1934.

[14] A study of farm labor, made during 1935–36 in the Yakima Valley, shows that the yearly cash income of 74 "transient" workers was considerably higher than the agricultural earnings shown in the study. The data from the Yakima Valley study cannot be compared directly with the data in this study because of the difference in the years (1933–34 against 1935–36) and the difference in scope of the studies. Nevertheless, it is interesting to observe that in the Yakima Valley, where wages are higher than in many other sections of the country, the authors found that "The largest percentage of both resident and transient (farm) workers received from $200 to $400 during the course of 1 year, although the percentage of residents falling in this income group is greater than for transients." See Landis and Brooks, op. cit.

For a distribution and average of yearly earnings, 1930 to 1935, among migrant family groups following agricultural employment, see Migratory Labor in California, State Relief Administration, Division of Special Surveys and Studies, San Francisco, 1936, p. 121.

TABLE 7.—MEDIAN NET YEARLY INCOME AND EMPLOYMENT PERIOD OF 500
MIGRATORY-CASUAL WORKERS, 1933–34

Type of worker	1933		1934	
	Median net yearly earnings	Median employment period (weeks)	Median net yearly earnings	Median employment period (weeks)
Agricultural	$110	23	$124	22
Industrial	257	26	272	24
Combination [1]	223	23	203	18

[1] Workers combining agricultural and industrial employment.

This comparison shows that in terms of averages the higher yearly earnings of workers employed entirely or partially in industry are not the result of a longer period of employment during the year. The obvious conclusion is that work in industrial processes is better paid than work in agriculture. However, it must be remembered that compact work patterns (see ch. II) are less frequent in industrial employment; therefore, the higher earnings may, in part, represent a differential necessary to insure an adequate supply of workers for operations involving a greater range of movement and a lesser certainty of recurrent employment.

The discussion in this chapter has been concerned with the general aspects of migratory-casual employment. This general discussion needs now to be supplemented by more detailed examinations. The employment characteristics of migratory-casual workers are conditioned by activities in a considerable number of particular crops and processes which behave in ways peculiar to themselves. A complete account of migratory-casual workers and their employment characteristics must consider these individual pursuits; and it is to such a consideration that the following chapter is devoted.

CHAPTER IV

TYPES OF MIGRATORY-CASUAL EMPLOYMENT

THE FACT THAT many crops and industries are dependent upon a supply of migratory-casual workers is, in each particular case, the result of a combination of conditions, none of which is static. As a result, the importance of the various crops and industries as sources of demand for migratory-casual labor is continually changing. At about the same time that the spread of cotton cultivation in California in the twenties was creating a new demand for migratory-casual labor, the use of the combine harvester caused a marked decrease in the number of migratory-casual workers needed in the wheat harvest. Mechanization frequently develops to the point where, as in the case of road, dam, and levee construction, the demand for manual laborers (e. g., pick-and-shovel men) is materially reduced. Much the same effect on the employment opportunities of the migratory-casual worker follows when the increase of population within one area provides a supply of resident workers for the jobs formerly filled by migrants.

In any case, the crops and industries which provided a substantial part of the migratory-casual employment during, say, a period of agricultural expansion, extensive railway construction, or the discovery of a new oil field, may decline rapidly in importance when this period is completed. It is difficult, then, to make generalizations about the specific sources of demand for migratory-casual labor that will hold true for more than a limited period of time. Certainly, it would be dangerous to attempt more than tentative conclusions on the basis of 500 work histories collected during the depression years, 1933 and 1934. The following description of migratory-casual employment in specific crops and industrial processes is therefore intended as no more than an account of the experience of a particular group of workers during a 2-year period. Despite their obvious limitations, the data in this section add measurably to an understanding of the part played by the migratory-casual worker in agriculture and industry.

AMOUNT OF EMPLOYMENT IN SPECIFIC CROPS AND PROCESSES

Agricultural Workers.

Among the 200 agricultural workers studied, the cotton crop was the largest single source of migratory-casual employment in 1933

and 1934 combined.[1] Slightly less employment was supplied by
the fruit and sugar-beet crops, followed, in the order of their importance, by grain, general farm work, vegetables, and berries (see
fig. 23).

That cotton should have headed this list is perhaps not altogether
to be expected, since the cotton crop, as an employer of migratory-
casual labor, has not generally received as much attention as grain,
fruit, and sugar beets.[2] The ranking position of cotton among the
agricultural workers in this study may be an outcome of the depression, or it may reflect the increasing importance of a crop in which
there has been but little replacement of manual labor by machines.
The importance of the fruit crops as employers of the workers studied
needs no emphasis. The position of the sugar-beet crop is equally
well known; it not only employs large numbers of migratory-casual
workers, but also provides a longer working season than any other
of the more important crops employing agricultural migrants. Indeed, the real importance of the sugar-beet industry as an employer
of migratory-casual labor is perhaps not adequately shown here,
since the workers studied were unattached men who may have been
handicapped in securing jobs in the beet fields in competition with an
adequate supply of the cheaper and more "reliable" family labor
preferred by employers.

The effect of the general adoption of the combine harvester upon
the demand for migratory-casual workers in the grain harvest is
reflected in the fact that, as figure 23 shows, grain was surpassed
by cotton, fruit, and sugar beets as an employer of the agricultural
workers studied. Despite the technological change in harvesting
wheat, however, it is important to note that in 1933 and 1934 the various grain crops remained 1 of the 4 chief employments of the 200
agricultural workers studied.

---

[1] Employment in the various pursuits is measured in terms of the total man-weeks employed for the 2 years 1933 and 1934. Employment in specific crops and industrial
processes for the 2 years is frequently combined in the discussions for two reasons:
(1) As appendix table 7 shows, there was a marked similarity in distribution of employment in the 2 years; and (2) the amount of information available for the somewhat
detailed descriptions of this section was increased by the combination without any
important loss in accuracy. The importance of cotton as a source of employment for
migratory-casual workers comes as much from the duration of the jobs as from the
number of persons it employs.

[2] Cotton is still usually thought of as a crop belonging exclusively to the Old South,
where great supplies of Negro labor are available. However, since 1910 there has been
a tremendous increase in cotton acreage and producuon in the Southwest, where the
absence of a supply of cheap resident labor makes the employment of migrants necessary.
Over one-half of the total cotton acreage (55 percent) and slightly less than one-half (48
percent) of the total production for the 1926–30 period was concentrated in the three
States of Arkansas, Oklahoma, and Texas; and California, New Mexico, and Arizona were
becoming increasingly important cotton producers. See Woofter, T. J., Jr., Landlord and
Tenant on the Cotton Plantation, Research Monograph V, Division of Social Research,
Works Progress Administration, Washington, D. C., 1936, pp. 38, 39; and Statistical
Abstract of the United States, 1935, pp. 624–626.

In comparison with the four crops which led in employment, the work secured in vegetables and berries was relatively much less important. Vegetables supplied about one-half as much employment as cotton, and because the jobs in berries were of short duration, they were somewhat less important than those in vegetables.

Work on general farms and on dairy and cattle farms represents, in part, off-season employment between jobs in the highly specialized and highly seasonal crops that have been discussed above. Jobs in general agriculture combined with jobs in dairy and cattle supplied only about as much work as had been secured in fruits alone. Employment in other crops—tobacco, grapes, hops, etc.—was of minor importance. Thus, excepting the off-season work, practically all the employment of the 200 agricultural workers was secured in 6 crops— cotton, fruits, sugar beets, grain, vegetables, and berries.

The description of specific agricultural pursuits as employers of the 200 agricultural workers has been, up to this point, in terms of the total man-weeks of work which each supplied. When, in contrast, the importance of specific crops is stated in terms of the *number* of jobs—a measure which should indicate roughly the relative numbers of workers employed in each at some time during the year, regardless of the length of their employment—a somewhat different arrangement occurs (see fig. 23). During 1933 and 1934 the fruit crop supplied the 200 agricultural workers with the greatest number of jobs, and probably gave employment, without regard to duration, to the greatest number of workers.[3] Cotton, which supplied the greatest amount of employment to the workers, was second in number of jobs supplied. Grain, which was fourth in amount of work, provided almost as many jobs as the cotton crop, and presumably affected almost as many workers, though for a shorter period of time.

The lack of agreement between the amount of employment and the number of jobs provided by the different pursuits indicates variations in the length of jobs in the various pursuits. Thus, jobs in sugar beets were relatively protracted, since, although only about one-half as numerous as jobs in grain, they provided considerably more employment. Jobs in vegetables and berries, on the other hand, are shown to have been of short duration, since they were more numerous than jobs in either sugar beets or general agriculture, yet were of minor importance in providing employment. In brief, a comparison of the number of jobs with the amount of employment, as shown in figure 23, reveals that the longest jobs were those in sugar beets, in general agriculture, and in dairy and cattle

---

[3] See footnote 1, p. 53, ch. III, for the definition of a "job" as used in this study.

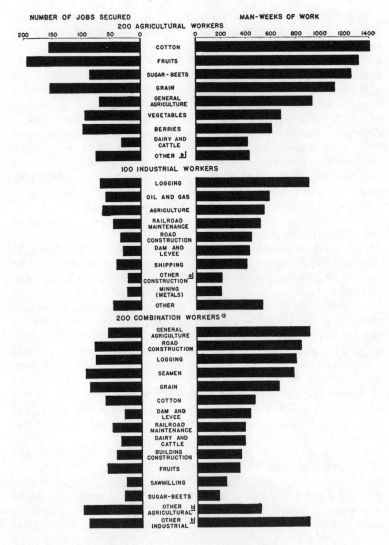

FIG. 23 – NUMBER OF JOBS AND MAN-WEEKS OF WORK
OF 500 MIGRATORY-CASUAL WORKERS
1933-1934 COMBINED

* Workers combining agricultural
and industrial employment

a] Tunnel, bridge, and building construction
b] Not elsewhere classified

AF 2378, W.P.A.

farming, and that the shortest were those in the sharply seasonal crops—berries, vegetables, grain, and fruits.

Industrial Workers.

Logging was the most important source of employment among the 100 industrial workers, in spite of the fact that it has probably been more affected than any other operation by decasualization consequent upon long-time and depression changes. In 1933 and 1934 logging supplied far more man-weeks of work than any other industry (see fig. 23). Somewhat less important than logging were oil and gas, agriculture,[4] and railroad maintenance. These pursuits, together with road, dam, and levee construction, and work as seamen, furnished practically all the employment secured by the 100 industrial workers. The remainder of their employment was furnished by other [5] construction, metal mining, sawmilling, and a miscellaneous assortment of pursuits of minor importance.

The fact that logging was the most important single industry in giving employment to the 100 workers suggests that it continues to be, in comparison with other industries, a large employer of migratory-casual labor. Yet it is well known that the decasualization of logging was far advanced as early as the late 1920's. The growth of urban areas adjacent to logging regions and the betterment of transportation facilities between the two made it possible, some years ago, for employers to begin replacing migratory-casual workers with more stable operatives who could settle their families close by, and the depression hastened this process. Nevertheless, the position of logging in providing employment for the 100 workers studied shows that migratory-casual workers, even at the bottom of the depression, could secure work in the logging camps.

The importance of the oil and gas industry in supplying work to the 100 industrial workers suggests a change in the character of the employments of migratory-casual workers, as mentioned earlier in the chapter. After logging operations had passed their peak and their need for migratory-casual workers was declining, new oil fields were opening up and creating a demand for migratory-casual workers.[6]

---

[4] The industrial workers in this study made frequent excursions into agriculture for employment. However, industrial employment was so much the rule among these workers that they are referred to for convenience as industrial rather than as principally industrial workers, which is a more exact description.

[5] Construction of tunnels, buildings, and bridges.

[6] The all-time high in lumber production occurred in 1909. At that time oil drilling produced only about one-sixth of the amount of petroleum that it produced in 1933. In 1933, lumber production was less than one-third of the 1909 production. See Statistical Abstract of the United States, 1935, pp. 661, 706. Of course, it is not suggested that the developing demand in drilling absorbed the unemployed migratory-casual workers from logging.

The relatively large amount of employment supplied by railroad maintenance is to be expected. Unskilled and low paid, requiring mobility and work in remote districts, section and extra-gang work has long been an important source of employment for migratory- casual workers. It was affected by the depression largely because railroad repair work was reduced to a minimum, rather than because the need declined.

Notable for the fact that they supplied the 100 industrial workers with little work during 1933–34 are: road construction, the construc- tion of tunnels, buildings, and bridges, the mining of metals, and sawmilling, all of which have at one time required great numbers of migratory-casual workers. It is highly probable that the position of these industries as indicated in figure 23 is the result of the conditions existing in 1933 and 1934. During the depression, road construction was to a large extent public work, hiring local unemployed and relief labor. Tunnel and bridge construction projects almost disappeared during the early years of the depression, and reappeared principally as public works in 1933. Mining and sawmilling both restricted their operation during the depression; moreover, both had been largely de- casualized before the depression began.

When the various industrial pursuits are rated on a basis of the number of jobs—rather than on the basis of man-weeks of employ- ment—the changes in order are small (see fig. 23). It appears, there- fore, that there was little variation among the different industrial pursuits in the average length of jobs. It may be observed, however, that such jobs as these workers obtained in agriculture were some- what shorter than those in the more important industries; and that the jobs in levee and dam construction tended to be somewhat longer than those in other pursuits.

Combination Workers.

The 200 workers whose employment combined agriculture and in- dustry found about equal amounts of employment in each. The single pursuit which furnished the greatest amount of employment was general agriculture, followed by road construction, logging, shipping, and grain (see fig. 23).

It will be observed that the order of the agricultural pursuits in providing work for the combination workers differs markedly from that described above for the strictly agricultural workers. Thus, general agriculture, which was the fifth most important pursuit of the strictly agricultural workers, is the most important pursuit of the present group; and grain, which was fourth when considered above, is the second most important agricultural pursuit of the combination workers.

These differences appear to indicate roughly which agricultural pursuits were most often combined with industrial work. Thus, as figure 23 shows, general farm work and work in grain were probably more often combined with industrial work than with other types of agricultural employment. The relatively small amount of employment in fruits and sugar beets among the combination workers is striking. It appears to be associated with the fact that habitual migratory-casual workers in fruit tend to confine themselves to the fruit harvest the year around, and with the fact that the peculiar nature of the sugar-beet season makes any combination of work with it difficult.[7]

Similarly, some industrial pursuits appear to be more easily combined with agricultural work. Road construction, which was relatively unimportant as a source of employment for the 100 industrial workers, is the most important industrial employment of the combination workers. On the other hand, oil and gas ranked second among the strictly industrial workers, but provided almost no employment to the combination group.

SEASONALITY OF EMPLOYMENT IN SPECIFIC CROPS AND PROCESSES

The total amount of employment obtained during 1933 and 1934, and the relationship of this total to the length of the migratory period were described for the 500 workers in chapter III. For a majority of the workers the employment season was short in relation to the migratory period and the full year. This short working season, of course, was the result of the fact that the types of jobs that were open to them—in agriculture, in industry, in combination employment—not only all tended to be highly seasonal, but also tended to reach peaks of employment at much the same time.

A study of particular activities in the three general types of employment which the workers followed helps to explain the shortness of the work season and the difficulty of dovetailing jobs to decrease the amount of working time lost. Very few of the pursuits afforded year-round employment. The majority of them were strongly seasonal, and most of them reached their peaks of employment activity between the months of May and September; during these 5 months the periods of greatest activity in the several pursuits overlapped in such a way that employment was concentrated within those few months.

---

[7] See the discussion of seasonality as it relates to sugar beets, p. 78. The sugar-beet season is difficult to combine with any other work, either industrial or agricultural. In addition, compare the number of stops made for jobs other than those in fruit and sugar beets as shown in the itineraries of the fruit and sugar-beet workers, figs. 6 and 7, ch. II.

Agricultural Workers.

Though infrequently reported, full-year employment sequences were possible in agriculture because of some degree of activity throughout the year in fruits, cotton, dairy and cattle, vegetables, and general agriculture. However, dairy and cattle, vegetables, and general agriculture (1933 only) were the only pursuits which could properly be termed year-round employment in the sense that their peak months were not strikingly higher than their low months and that their employment curves were flattened out over a large proportion of the year (see fig. 24). Of these three, only general agriculture ranked among the five most important pursuits for agricultural workers in the 2 years combined (see appendix tables 7 and 8).

Eight of the nine principal pursuits in which agricultural migratory-casual workers were engaged showed definite peaks of employment activity of varying degrees of sharpness in both years. One of the crops, vegetables, had a clearly marked double peak of activity; and in another crop, sugar beets, the high point of activity resembles a plateau extending through all the summer months. The extent to which activity in the more important crops overlapped is indicated by the fact that the high points of employment in fruits, grain, hops, and vegetables (in 1933) occurred in 3 months, July through September.

Cotton was the only one of the five leading employments whose peak months did not overlap those of other important pursuits; activity reached a high point in October in both 1933 and 1934. Fruits, with maximum employment reached in the period June through September, overlapped grain. Employment in both fell away sharply on either side of these peak months. Employment in sugar beets remained at the same high level from May to September, overlapping both grain and fruits, and declined to almost nothing during the rest of the year. Although general agriculture in 1933 provided some work during the winter, it nevertheless showed a definite peak in May and somewhat overlapped fruits and sugar beets. Of the minor pursuits, berries were active from May to August 1934, and the entire hop season occurred in September of both years.

In summary, it may be said that of the five most important agricultural pursuits only one, general agriculture in 1933, provided. anything approaching a year-round level of employment. The others were sharply peaked in the 6 months between May and October, and the overlapping of their peaks tended to concentrate employment in the summer period. In addition, two minor crops, berries (in 1934) and hops, reached their peaks during the same 6-month period.

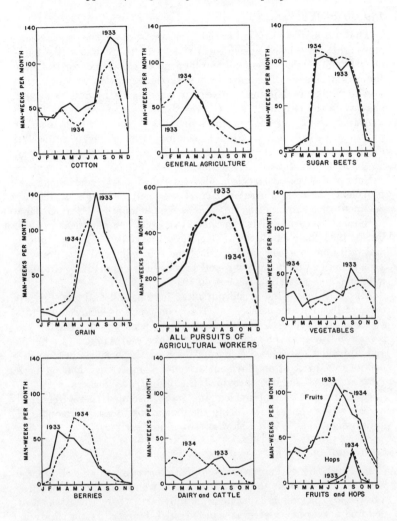

FIG.24 – SEASONAL FLUCTUATION OF EMPLOYMENT IN ALL
AND IN SELECTED PURSUITS
200 AGRICULTURAL WORKERS
1933-1934

AF-2382, W.P.A.

Industrial Workers.

The employment of industrial workers showed the same sharp seasonality as that of agricultural workers. There was a like tendency for but little year-round employment to exist, and for the more important sources of employment, with the exception of logging, to rise to high, overlapping, midyear peaks of activity and to decline sharply in the late months of the year.

Among the 5 most important industrial pursuits, which together provided the greater part of all the employment of the 100 industrial migratory-casual workers, only 1, gas and oil in 1933, furnished an appreciable amount of year-round employment.

Dam and levee construction also furnished fairly continuous employment during the greater part of the year, although its activity declined for a short period during the winter months. Seamen (few in number) secured fairly consistent year-round employment in 1934, but in 1933 their employment fluctuated markedly. Bridge, tunnel, and building construction furnished the 100 industrial workers with a very small amount of year-round employment opportunity throughout 1933, and only slightly more in 1934.

All of the major industrial pursuits—logging, oil and gas, agriculture, railroad maintenance, and road construction—showed definite seasonal peaks in both years. Most of the peak activity during the 2 years fell within the months of June, July, and August (see fig. 25 and appendix table 9). Logging alone of the major pursuits did not reach a peak of employment activity in midyear. During both 1933 and 1934 logging provided the industrial workers with the greatest amount of employment in March, declined thereafter until it reached its annual low during the dangerous forest fire months of midsummer, then began a slow rise to winter activity.

Combination Workers.

Although the workers in the combination group had a much greater variety of jobs than those in the other two groups and were less affected by pronounced peaks in employment, their work was still definitely seasonal and was concentrated largely in the midyear period (see fig. 26 and appendix table 10). This group of workers had more employment in the winter and spring than did the agricultural group, but much less in the early fall and summer, even though the most active months for employment were June in 1933 and July in 1934.

Although the 200 migratory-casual workers who combined agricultural with industrial employment have been treated as a separate— a *combination*—group in this analysis, the specific jobs they held were much the same as those described in the discussion of the 200

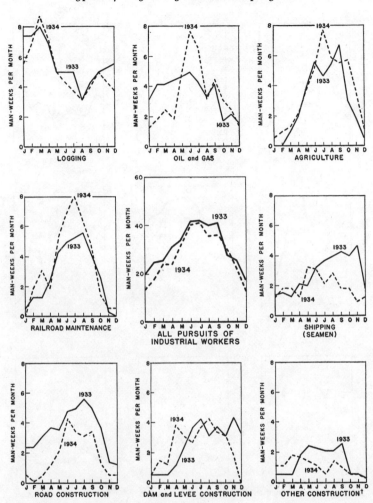

FIG. 25 – SEASONAL FLUCTUATION OF EMPLOYMENT IN ALL
AND IN SELECTED PURSUITS
100 INDUSTRIAL WORKERS
1933 - 1934

† Tunnel, Bridge, and Building Construction

AF-2376, W.P.A.

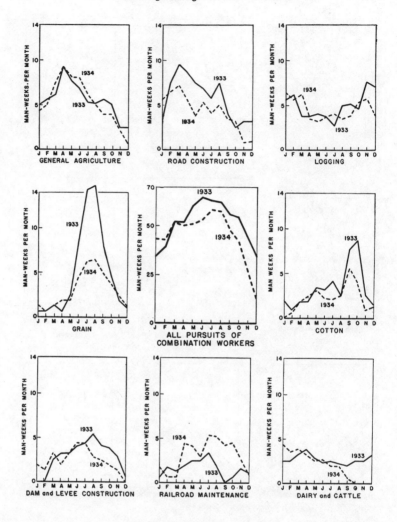

F<small>IG.</small> 26 – SEASONAL FLUCTUATION OF EMPLOYMENT IN ALL
AND IN SELECTED PURSUITS
200 COMBINATION WORKERS*
1933-1934

\# Workers combining Agricultural and Industrial Employments

AF-2380, W.P.A.

agricultural and the 100 industrial workers. Thus, the separate classification was necessary, not because the work done was different, but because these 200 individuals were not attached solely, or principally, to either agriculture or industry during the years 1933 and 1934.

The fact that these workers were, in a sense, "free lances", because they did not appear to be attached to either agriculture or industry, undoubtedly affected the number and duration of their jobs; but, as can be seen from figure 26, the jobs that provided the most employment were those that have already been discussed. It would seem, therefore, that little additional information would be gained on the nature of specific migratory-casual employments from a description of the jobs held by the 200 combination workers. The essential information on the jobs held by these workers is presented in figure 26; and the earlier discussion of these same types of employment applies, in general, to these workers also.

1934 CHANGES IN SPECIFIC CROPS AND PROCESSES

In presenting information on the amount and the seasonality of the employment of migratory-casual workers in various pursuits, the general similarity of data for the years 1933 and 1934 has been noted. In sugar beets, cotton, railroad maintenance, and logging (see figs. 24, 25, 26), the 1934 seasonal variations were practical duplications of those of 1933. However, for some crops and processes there were differences both in the amount of employment and in the seasonal variations; these differences appear to be the result of special factors operating during 1 of the 2 years.

Factors that probably affected agricultural employment in 1934 were the drought and the crop-reduction program. Evidence of the effect of these factors is to be found in the striking reduction in the amount of employment in grain; the drop in the amount of employment in cotton in 1934; and the increase in the importance of berry picking and general farming jobs during 1934, which suggests that workers were forced to take less desirable jobs because of the reduction in grain and cotton employment.

There were exceptions, also, to the general agreement of amount and seasonality of employment among industrial workers. Road construction declined in importance during 1934 as compared with 1933 because such construction depended so much upon public works and relief grants designed to provide jobs for the resident unemployed. Railroad maintenance, on the contrary, increased in importance as a source of employment, probably because transportation lines began to make badly needed repairs to their right-of-ways.

This chapter, in addition to presenting more detailed information on the particular jobs that migratory-casual workers follow, contributes to an understanding of why the supply of workers is generally in excess of the number that can be given employment at any time. The seasonal peaks of activity in agricultural and industrial employments are so sharp in contrast to the troughs, and there is such a concentration of activity within a few months in the summer and fall, that clearly a labor supply large enough to meet these peak demands must of necessity go unemployed during much of the year. This bunching of demand in a few months makes employment sequences covering the year extremely difficult to obtain. The most remarkable thing about the amount of employment secured during the year, pitiably small as it has been shown to be, is that so much employment was obtained under the circumstances. One explanation of how the workers managed to extend the period of employment in highly seasonal operations is that they traveled with the seasons, taking all possible advantage of the fact that climate and geography alter the timing of even the most seasonal of employments.

CHAPTER V

SOME PERSONAL CHARACTERISTICS

THERE ARE TWO reasons for reserving until near the end of this report a discussion of some of the personal characteristics of the 500 migratory-casual workers studied. First, there is the belief stated in chapter I that although the migratory-casual worker is the result of a combination of economic and personal factors, the economic factors are of principal importance, and therefore should be considered first. Second, there is the fact that data on personal characteristics must be qualified to a greater extent than has been necessary up to this point, because of the bias occasioned by the method of selecting workers for study. In choosing cases, preference was given to those with complete work histories, and consequently there was a tendency to include only the more successful workers. This preference undoubtedly affects the distribution of personal-characteristics data.

Earlier chapters have presented the more important discussions of the general nature of the migratory-casual worker, his position in the labor market, the extent of his wanderings, the kind and amount of work he does, and the earnings that he derives from his efforts. At this point it should be interesting and valuable to consider some of his personal characteristics. This will be done quantitatively in terms of data on age, color and nativity, and years spent in migratory-casual employment. And it will be done qualitatively in terms of selected personal histories.

YEARS SPENT IN MIGRATORY-CASUAL LABOR

Just when a migrant becomes a confirmed migratory-casual worker cannot be determined with any pretense of accuracy. The worker who leaves a settled residence because of economic conditions, personal difficulties, or any one of a dozen motivating forces usually takes to the road as a means of escaping a situation over which he believes he has no control. Migration is a time-honored and, frequently, an effective device for "changing your luck"; and more often than not it is a temporary expedient. During the depression, thousands of persons became transients for relatively short periods of time;[1] but

---

[1] See Webb, John N., The Transient Unemployed, Research Monograph III, Division of Social Research, Works Progress Administration, Washington, D. C., 1936, p. 64 ff.

only a small proportion of them found life on the road as satisfactory in experience as it had seemed in prospect. Among the many who set out in good times and bad, some would-be migrants get no farther than their first impulse carries them; others go on for months in a state of semiadaptation; while a small proportion drifts slowly into an irrevocable attachment to life on the road.

Because this study of the confirmed migratory-casual worker was made at a time of social unrest when thousands of temporary migrants were moving about the country, it was essential to select individuals who clearly had made a complete break with the sedentary way of life. There were two tests which, if applied jointly, would distinguish the habitual from the temporary migrant: (1) a livelihood that depended upon short-time seasonal or intermittent employments at casual pursuits, joined with (2) at least 1 year of migration immediately preceding the time this study was made. Actually, as table 8 shows, the great majority of the 500 workers in this report were veterans of the road—men who had "learned the ropes" before the depression brought temporary recruits by the tens of thousands.

TABLE 8.—YEARS SPENT IN MIGRATORY-CASUAL WORK BY 500 WORKERS

Years spent in migratory-casual work	Total	Type of worker		
		Agricultural	Industrial	Combination [1]
All workers	500	200	100	200
		Percent distribution		
All workers	100	100	100	100
Less than 1 year				
1 to 2 years	3	4	2	2
2 to 4 years	17	18	14	17
4 to 6 years	14	17	10	14
6 to 8 years	10	11	8	10
8 to 10 years	9	8	10	9
10 to 15 years	16	16	16	17
15 to 20 years	12	10	17	11
20 years or more	18	15	23	19
Not ascertainable	1	1		1

[1] Workers combining agricultural and industrial employment.

Nearly half of the 500 workers had followed migratory-casual pursuits for 10 years or longer, and a substantial proportion for 20 or more years. Workers following industrial employment had the greatest proportion of "old timers", and agricultural workers the least. However, the importance of table 8 lies not in the distribution of workers by years of service, but in the clear evidence that the 500 workers were habitual migrants who are not to be confused with the depression transient or with the nonworking tramp.

AGE

The fact that workers were selected for study on a basis of clearly demonstrated service in the ranks of the migratory-casual worker must be kept in mind when examining the age data presented in table 9. Both the young (under 20 years) and the old (65 years and over) were few in number. The proportion of younger persons was directly affected by the selection of workers with at least a full year on the road and enough employment to allow classification by type of employment; this procedure tended to exclude all but a few migratory-casual workers under 20 years of age. The small number of individuals 65 years and over is also the result of a selective process; but in this case it is the natural process of selection imposed by the strenuous life that migratory-casual workers lead.

TABLE 9.—AGE OF 500 MIGRATORY-CASUAL WORKERS

Age	Total	Type of worker		
		Agricultural	Industrial	Combination [1]
All workers	500	200	100	200
	Percent distribution			
All workers	100	100	100	100
15 to 19 years	1	1	----------	1
20 to 24 years	10	12	11	8
25 to 29 years	16	15	10	20
30 to 34 years	16	14	21	16
35 to 44 years	28	25	30	31
45 to 54 years	18	17	20	18
55 to 64 years	9	13	7	5
65 years or over	2	3	1	1

[1] Workers combining agricultural and industrial employment.

Most of the 500 workers were between the ages of 20 and 45— age limits within which the unskilled worker's efforts are most productive. Comparable age data from a study of the depression transient indicate that the 500 migratory-casual workers of this report were older than the depression transient, but younger than the resident (local) homeless population [2] of the large cities.

---

[2] Resident or local homeless persons are a distinct and identifiable group in all large cities. They are to be found on the streets and in the subways, in the municipal lodging houses, the missions, the Salvation Army soup kitchens, and in the "shantytowns"; weather permitting, they can be seen along the docks and in the parks. Certain sections of the large cities are known as their habitat; for instance, the Bowery in New York City, the

Group	Median age	45 years and over
Unattached transients [1]	27 to 30 years	12 to 16 percent
500 migratory-casual workers	37 years	29 percent
Local homeless persons [1]	42 to 45 years	40 to 49 percent

[1] Represents the range of monthly values during the period October 1934 through April 1935. See The Transient Unemployed, op. cit. p. 29.

The reasons for these differences in age are readily found. Transients were newcomers among the mobile labor group; they came principally from among the younger group of the unemployed resident population; and about one-half of them remained on the road for 6 months or less. In contrast, the 500 migratory-casual workers in this study were chosen on a basis of clearly defined work patterns involving at least a full year of migration. Even though some few depression transients were included in this selection, it was only in those cases where the process of adaptation to the life of the confirmed migrant had gone far enough to leave little question that the worker would remain on the road. The local homeless of the cities are made up largely of men who have been wanderers of one sort or another but who have been forced by age or physical disabilities to abandon the strenuous life on the road.

COLOR AND NATIVITY

The native-white migratory-casual worker supplies the greater part of the labor force needed for seasonal and intermittent jobs, despite efforts to obtain a cheaper and more tractable supply of foreign-born workers.[3] Among the 500 migratory-casual workers included in this study, the native-white group represented about three-quarters of the total, the foreign-born group—white, Oriental, and Mexican—about one-sixth, and the Negro group, one-twentieth (see table 10). Because of limitations imposed by the selection of the cases for study, these proportions should be used only as a rough indication of the relative importance of the different color and nativity groups in the total migratory-casual labor supply.

The color and nativity characteristics of the three types of workers in table 10 show the Mexican to be a more important element among workers following agricultural employment than among those fol-

---

"Slave-Market" at West Madison and South State Streets in Chicago, and the "Skidroad" in Seattle. These sections, of course, are also frequented by migratory-casual workers. Although most of the resident homeless group are casual laborers when they work, and although many of them leave the city for short periods of time, they are not migratory-casual workers in the sense employed in this report. Rather, they are a "home guard" that exists precariously on panhandling, odd jobs, the missions, and city institutions for the unattached resident homeless.

[3] The use of Oriental and Mexican workers was discussed on p. 12 ff.

lowing industrial, or a combination of types of employment. It is probable that the actual percentages were biased by the fact that two of the cities in which interviews were made—Denver and Minneapolis—are in sugar-beet areas where the Mexican worker is an important element in the labor supply for that crop. Other studies [4] have shown that the Mexican is extensively used in industrial employments, such as railroad right-of-way maintenance, and it is likely that the Mexican migratory-casual worker in industry was underrepresented in this study. None the less, the indication in table 10 that Mexicans are more frequently· found in agricultural than in industrial employment is believed to be a correct statement of the order of importance.

TABLE 10.—COLOR AND NATIVITY OF 500 MIGRATORY-CASUAL WORKERS

Color and nativity	Total	Type of worker		
		Agricultural	Industrial	Combination [1]
All workers	500	200	100	200
	Percent distribution			
All workers	100	100	100	100
White	85	78	91	90
Native	77	73	80	81
Foreign-born	8	5	11	9
Negro	5	5	3	5
Mexican	9	15	6	4
Others	1	2	----------	1

[1] Workers combining agricultural and industrial employment.

The small proportion of Negroes among the migratory-casual workers studied is a reflection of the fact that for them employment opportunities on the road are limited. Moreover, the Negro has, traditionally, been an immobile group in the population. The only striking example of migration of Negroes in recent years was the movement of southern Negroes to the industrial centers of the North during and after the World War as the result of extensive recruiting activities to supply a cheap labor supply for the heavy industries.

Racial prejudice commonly operates as a check on the mobility of Negroes by increasing the difficulties of travel, and by limiting the number of job opportunities. The Negro who travels by highway or freight train is more likely to encounter overstrict interpretation of the vagrancy laws than is the white migrant, and racial prejudice on the part of some employers and many workers places the Negro

[4] See footnote 7, p. 42.

at a competitive disadvantage in finding employment in some parts of the country. An interesting example of deliberately restricted employment opportunities is to be found in a report which states that in several southern States, employment agencies sending Negroes out of the State for migratory labor assignments were practically taxed out of existence.[5]

It will be recalled that the maps in chapter II showing routes of travel (by crops and industrial processes) had few lines running into the States of the Old South. In these States, where the Negro is most numerous, he provides a ready supply of cheap labor for agricultural and, to an important but lesser extent, for industrial operations that otherwise would require a mobile labor reserve for seasonal and intermittent peaks of activity.

PERSONAL HISTORIES

The principal advantage of the foregoing statistical description is that a few of the personal characteristics of all the 500 workers can be viewed at one time. The principal disadvantage of this procedure is that the results fail to show, or even to suggest, the distinctive personality of any of these workers. Without some indication of what they are as individuals, this report would fall short of its purpose of describing, in terms of economic and personal factors, the confirmed migratory-casual worker.

The purely personal factor will be presented through the device of brief histories, some of them abstracted from the field interviewer's report on the worker, and some of them in the worker's own words, edited solely for length. Since only a few of the available 500 histories could be included, a selection was made of those that seemed to represent attitudes, habits, and personalities of frequent occurrence among the entire group, and, it is believed, among confirmed migratory-casual workers in general.

Wanderlust.

The constant urge to be on the move, the tendency to treat employment as a means of gratifying this urge, and the real or fancied independence of the migratory-casual worker are illustrated by the personal histories of Jack Lamb, John McClosky, and Harry Burnside.[6]

---

[5] "In Alabama a license fee of $2,500 was required, and an additional amount up to 50 percent of this sum might be levied in each county of the State in which the private agency operated. * * * A bond of $5,000 was required in each county." Harrison, Shelby M., and Associates, Public Employment Offices, Russell Sage Foundation, New York, 1924, p. 86. Moreover, "efforts of citizens to prevent Negro recruiting [for out-of-State employment] went as far as threats of violence to the recruiting agent", p. 606.

[6] The names here, and throughout this section, are fictitious.

Jack Lamb, 32 years old, a Cherokee Indian, began work in the gas and oil fields after he left the Navy in 1926. By following pipeline construction and repair jobs throughout Texas and Oklahoma, Mr. Lamb was able to remain employed a good part of the time, despite the short duration of most of the jobs he secured.

His largest yearly earnings at this work were $900, made in 1929. Since that time he had earned considerably less, but never less than $250. In 1934, a fairly typical year for his employment, he held three jobs: one in Duval County, Tex., lasting 1 month; the second in Victoria, Tex., lasting 5 months; and a third at Refugio, Tex., lasting 2 weeks. His earnings for the year were $550.

Jack Lamb went into migratory-casual work because it appealed to him. Not liking confinement to a single job or place, he prefers pipeline work to any other because it allows him to leave a job whenever he wishes, and to obtain another without much difficulty. His frequent periods of unemployment are not unwelcome, for he is extremely fond of fishing and gambling. Mr. Lamb's earnings have nearly always been adequate for his needs; and if necessary, he could usually borrow from other pipe-line workers. Accordingly he has rarely sought relief.

Autobiography of John McClosky

Born in Missouri in 1889. Went to Illinois in covered wagon along with father, mother, three sisters, two brothers. Father ran hoist at coal mine, traded horses, peddled fish, crockery, and did jobs of work around Peoria, Ill. About 1893 my mother and one sister died of typhoid fever. Dad came to Seattle. Built and lived in one-room shack at foot of Kinnear Park. Moved to 6 miles north of Bellingham. On this place I begin to do hard labor, helped saw stove wood. I hauled wood to Bellingham and peddled it. Then I got a job as bellboy in Byron Hotel (was awfully green) then went to work for Western Union, messenger boy.

Ran away from home. Went to Seattle and got a job as deckboy on steamship that went to San Francisco. I got paid off there, got taken in by sights of the big city. Came to my senses, my boat had sailed. I had 5¢ left in my pocket. I spent it for a newspaper and looked through the ads. Porter wanted, Restaurant. Convinced the boss I could do the work, $5 a week and board. Stayed there 10 days, had fight with cook, got fired. Got a job on a steamer to San Diego. Worked 3 months then quit. Got a job in a family hotel in San Francisco as bellboy, stayed there 3 weeks and got fired for pulling a boner. Went back to San Diego. Left after short time. Got job in Hotel San Rafael, San Francisco, bellboy, $15 per month.

About this time I began to think of home for the first time. After 4 weeks I wrote home. Dad had moved to near Blaine, Wash., on 40 acres of unimproved land. Headed for home. Went to Aberdeen on a lumber schooner, Seattle on train, to Blaine on the boat. Stayed awhile. Struck out for Seattle. Got job as flunkey in logging camp. Never stayed long in one place. Get few dollars, go to Seattle, go broke—then go back and work some more. After a while I would get sick. Go home. Stay a short time. Gone again.

I finally got work in a new shingle mill near my father's ranch. I worked there in the woods cutting shingle bolts, and learning to saw and pack shingles. Then I went to Everett, Wash., and lived around there cutting shingle bolts, sawing, and packing. Worked in shingle mills up and down Puget Sound. Never stayed long in one place. I put in 3 years on Vancouver Island sawing shingles. Spent most of my winters on a trap line in Whatcom County, near my father's ranch.

In 1918 I married (May 3). Wife and I came to Seattle and I longshored up to the general strike in 1919. Drove a car for my brother-in-law for 18 months. Went east of the mountains logging. Back to Seattle. Peddled hand-bills from house to house. Worked for junk company. Cut wood on the beach. Worked on a paving job, wheeling sand and gravel to the concrete mixer.

My wife's health was poorly, and they said the mountain air would help her. I went up to Lake Wenatchee to cut shingle bolts and took my wife. Stayed there 2 years while my wife's health greatly improved. Picked apples in Wenatchee Valley for the first time. Wife wanted divorce. Started same then changed mind. After another year took another notion for divorce. I went to San Juan Island and cut cordwood from January to August. When I came out to Bellingham I found I was divorced.

I worked 2 months mucking on the Cascade Tunnel. Sawed shingles at Quilcene, Wash. Worked one winter for a coal company in Seattle. Made cedar shakes one summer at Kerriston, Wash. Was married while there. Wife and I parted same year. Since then I have been knocking around Washington working here and there at odd jobs, mostly in the Wenatchee Valley but I have only averaged 4 months work per year since 1928.

Harry Burnside, 40 years old, has been a logger, Great Lakes seaman, harvest hand, general farm laborer, and itinerant peddler in every State from Illinois to Washington. Largely as a result of his experiences he had become a remarkably independent and self-reliant person, jealous of his rights and, except in the worst of times, capable of taking care of himself. Mr. Burnside supplied the following account of his wanderings from January 1, 1933, to February 18, 1935 :

Minneapolis, Jan. 1, 1933 by street-car to White Bear Minnesota by buss to Stillwater from Stillwater walked payd fare and rode freight to Madison, Wis. When I arrived in Madison Feb. 2 1933 i had accumulated about seven dollars in cash. i rented a room and boght some paint and other material and made some articles to sell but to my distress the chamber of comirce and the Police notified me that i have to pay 5 dollars permit (the five dollars which i dint have) so after eating a bowl of soup at the relieff station i took my bundles of unsold goods and mounted a blind of Milwaukee passenger train headed for Watertown Wis. when i arrived in Watertown in 2 below zero Weather a brave citysen (his name is motercicle Mike) told me to stay on because the dint want no one without money in this town so i stayed on to nex division. from there i went to Oshkosh Wis by freight. same thing there so i rode a freyght to Fond du Lac where i sold my goods [celluloid novelty piris and rings].

i took a freyght from state of Wis and rode to Margaret Iowa from Margaret to Freeport Ill by way of Dubuque Davenport and Moline by freyght and buss. in Freeport i met a man with a car selling cleaner. i made a deal with him to stand half expenses and change off driving. both of us got along pretty well, for a while so went back by way of Moline Rock Island etc to Omaha Neb when we arrived in Omaha it was about midle of March 1933 so we stayed in Omaha about 45 days and things went well. from Omaha we went to Aberdeen S. Dak. where our car broke down. my frend sold it. for 7 dollars and went home. we had saved during our travels 72 dollars each. i went to Minniapolis with intentions to buy myself an old Ford but could not make a satisfactory deal and it was getting late in August so i decided to visit my sister in Chicago.

i had a few dollars left but not enough to travel as people should so i rode freyght back to Chicago expecting to get work of some kind (being under the Elusion of the New administration) but in Chicago i dint get emploiment or find my sister, so discurraged and disappointed i had to leave chicago pedling baskets and what not towards the northwest. when i arrived in Duluth in November i was in hopes to get work in the woods but all those i had worked for prevous had shut down or went out of Operation entirely. so i went to minniapolis to winter. i stayed around there until May 15, 1934 (during that time i spent 4 months in the Minniapolis Penal Institution for trying to keep above the grave) i left Minniapolis by fregt train to Fargo to Grand Forks to Devils Lake to Minot to Kenmore to Egeland to Devils Lake to Caselton to Valley City to Jamestown to Bismark to Glendive Mont. Miles City to Forsyth to Helena to Misula to Sand Point to Spokane las week in October. Spokane to Yakima to Auburn to Tacoma. stayd in Tacoma 3 weeks selling willow baskets. Tacoma to Seattle by boat staid there 7 weeks Seattle to Portland by fregt. 2 weeks there. Back to Tacoma for Chrismas and came by bus to Seattle. Been here ever since.

Occupational and Physical Deterioration.

The long-time effects of the migratory-casual life upon the workers could hardly be expected to be other than injurious. Since the work is largely unskilled, any specialized occupational fitness the workers may have had is likely to deteriorate through disuse. Many of the workers studied had suffered in this way; typical cases of deterioration of skill are those of Joe McMathews and Tony Slotnig.

Physically, the effects of migratory-casual workers are likely to be even more disastrous. Inadequate shelter and diet, strenuous work under conditions often unhealthful, and lack of medical care, all contribute to the premature superannuation that is characteristic of many of the workers over 40 years. Evidence of physical deterioration are to be found in the cases of John Peterson and Jesús Lopez.

Joe McMathews, 46, was the son of a well-to-do Ohio farmer. During his junior year in college he had a violent quarrel with his father "over abusing a horse", and as a result left home. Soon afterward he married and moved to San Francisco. There he obtained a job in a seed house, and was soon promoted to one of more responsibility, his knowledge of agriculture standing him in good stead. His wife, however, did not like California, and her insistence that he quit his job and return to the Middle West finally resulted in a quarrel and divorce.

After his divorce, Mr. McMathews left the seed house and drifted into less stable jobs, such as skilled cannery work and crew boss in the vineyards. In 1923, he went into politics and got an appointment as a county highway inspector at $14 a day, but lost the job 9 months later, following an election. He said that he regretted ever having gone into politics because it had given him a taste for an easy job at big pay and spoiled him.

Failing to get another political job, he became a migratory-casual worker, and with the exception of 1 year spent in operating a rented orchard and a second year spent as a faro dealer in a Los Angeles gambling house, he had remained one ever since. His migrations had carried him to jobs in nearly all the Mountain and Middle Western States. He had been an oil-field worker, a wheat, lettuce, and fruit harvester, a bricklayer, a truck driver, a cannery worker, a cornhusker, a tie cutter, a houseman in a pool hall, a berry picker, and a trapper. During this period his unskilled jobs became more and more frequent until, by 1934, he was reduced mainly to picking berries and trapping.

When interviewed, Mr. McMathews was "stoically patient" about accepting his "present condition" and was busy making plans for the future on the basis of recognition of "past mistakes", that is, his wandering life during the last decade. He believed that he could establish himself as an influential member of a "respectable" community. The interviewer remarked that Mr. McMathews' optimism was probably due to the fact that he intended to return to Ohio in the spring to marry a childhood sweetheart who had just inherited a large, fertile farm upon the death of her father.

Joe McMathews had "definitely concluded" that the depression would continue only 1 year longer.

Autobiography of Tony Slotnig

I was born in Ohio. My folks took me back to the old country [Austria] when I was a baby and I don't know why. My father worked in the vineyards, and I did too. I kept running away from home and working. My uncle wrote me about how fine everything was over in America, and I came over here and found it wasn't so fine. (Oh yes, I did make good money, but that's all gone now.)

I first went to work in an iron foundry at Verona, Pa., for $1.75 a day. Then I got a big job with an insulator company doing piece work, trimming insulators. I was making as high as $10 a day. I was young and full of hell and went into the city every night, got drunk, stayed out all night, and would come back to work in the morning too sleepy to see. The inspector would come along, take a look at an insulator and throw it into the scrap heap. I told him not to do it and got mad and hit him over the head with one. He chased me and I ran and when we passed the cashier's window my check was already waiting for me.

Then the papers came out all about the big wages Henry Ford was paying, and I got hungry for that. Packed up and went to Detroit. Found that everybody there was a mechanic. Worked at common labor until I could buy some tools, then worked for Ford for 13 months at $5.60 a day during the war. I quit him because there wasn't enough money in it. Went back to Detroit and worked as a machinist.

In 1924 I met my wife and got married with her. I worked at piece work in the Fisher Body Plant, getting as high as $20 a day. In 1926 I went to work for the U. S. Radio Corporation at $1.50 an hour. In 1929 I got my arm caught and tore up the muscles in it. I was sick 4 or 5 months. My wife was in the family way and we had one hell of a time. I signed a petition I was o. k. and went back to work for 2 months in 1930, then they laid me off because there wasn't enough work. I had slowed down because my hand got numb when I tried to use it and I couldn't grasp a lathe like I used to. I had the case reopened twice trying to get more damages, but the company had smarter fellows than I had.

Well, my wife went back to her folks. They forclosed the mortgage on our house. My wife's brother-in-law and sister had to move in with the old folks too, making nine of us in the little house. Her folks didn't like me and said I was a foreigner and a Catholic and didn't have any education. I packed up and left. They had me arrested for deserting my family, and made me work for the relief and report to the judge every week. I couldn't stick it, so came out west in 1933.

I hitch-hiked through the Dakotas, inquired in a pool hall for a job, and found one on a farm plowing for 50¢ a day. Worked there 8 weeks and never got but $4. Was walking around the street hungry when I met a fellow half drunk who told me about a job he was supposed to go to that I could have if I wanted it. I sure was lucky he was drunk. I harvested there, and made about $60. Then I went to Colorado to work in the sugar beets, but nothing there but Mexicans. I got a job cutting grapes for Filipino contractors. They hire more men than they need so they can collect for boarding them. We had rice three times a day and slept on the floor like hogs. I think I owed them board when I left. It was terrible there and if the government doesn't believe it, I've got the man's name here on a card and you can go see for yourself. [He produced a card with the name and address of the vineyard owner on it.]

I started to pick cotton but heard that there was a big strike on and two people killed, so I got cold feet and left the country. Had a dish-washing job for a fellow who got sick, but he was only sick a week. Then I hit the freight and got in a good job of harvesting at Colfax, Wash. I tried to pick apples, but couldn't find anything. Went to Moxie, Wash. and picked hops and sure made it good—about $25 in two weeks; slipped in lots of leaves in the bottom of the sack. I found a farm job where I have been ever since. They expected me to milk 6 cows and kept piling on more work, all for just tobacco money, so I quit. I'll do most anything I can find, though. Think I'll stay in Washington, because if you go to California, you can't get nothing to do unless you are a Filipino or a native son.

Jesús Lopez, 50-year-old Mexican, came to the United States with his family in 1916. During the first 3 years of his stay he did extragang work on various Middle Western railroads. In 1919–20 the possibility of larger earnings through the employment of his wife and children caused him to leave extra-gang work to take his family to the Texas cottonfields.

He and his family separated and he worked again in extra gangs until, in 1924, he took the usual migratory-casual method of protesting against bad conditions—quitting the job. After 4 years of work in sugar beets (1924–28) he had secured a steady job as a section hand near Broken Bow, Nebr.

Jesús Lopez lost this job in 1931, when he was 47. "They tell me I am too old", he said. Unable to get railroad work again, he turned to the beet fields like many other migratory-casual workers who were judged to be too old for industrial occupations. After 1932 he had worked mostly in sugar beets, with some apple picking.

Jesús Lopez had not earned more than $75 in any 1 year after 1932. His highest earnings (in 1922) were $500. Since 1928 he had made his headquarters in Seattle, where he ordinarily spends July to September and December to May. When interviewed, he was living in Seattle's shantytown, "Hooverville", and had been spending his spare time collecting junk to sell and hunting firewood.

John Peterson, 55 years old and in poor health, came to America from Sweden when he was 20. In Sweden he had been a farm laborer, and he continued with the same work in America, spending his time in the Dakotas and in Minnesota doing seasonal farm work— plowing, haying, and threshing wheat. In between times he worked at road construction, street repairs in Fargo and Minneapolis, as a general farm hand in various places in the Northwest, and as a logger in northern Minnesota. During all this time he had periods of ill health caused by an early illness and aggravated by the rigors of his migratory life. An especially serious illness followed an accident in which his leg was broken.

A combination of harvest work with logging and construction had provided him with adequate employment up until 1932, but in 1933 he secured only 3 weeks of harvest work at Fargo, and spent the rest of the year idle. In 1934 he had had three jobs, which together lasted less than 6 months; in the spring he had gone to northern Minnesota as a logger and earned $1 a day for 4 months; late in the summer he had 1 month of work hauling grain; and shortly before being interviewed he had worked for a week shoveling snow in Minneapolis. He had just refused a job in a logging camp paying 35 cents a day.

Throughout his 25 years of migratory-casual work, Mr. Peterson has been in the habit of spending the winter idle in Minneapolis, except for short portions of a few winters spent in logging. However, the mode of living which the miserable earnings of his migratory work forced him to follow had undermined his health so completely that he was forced at last to leave for a warmer climate. When interviewed, he was en route to Texas, where he had some hope that his health would become improved. He wished to spend the rest of his life in a warmer climate.

John Peterson was very gloomy during the interview. He declared that there would never be any more seasonal work available in the wheat harvest, and that the future was "very dark" for all men of his type. He was unmarried, and thought this situation fortunate inasmuch as he is no longer able to find enough work even to support himself.

Attitude Towards Relief.

In general, the habitual migratory-casual worker applied for relief only when there was no alternative. Pride in his ability to care for himself, and a dislike of the routine of relief procedures—interviews, delays, and a scheduled way of living—kept him out of transient bureaus except for an occasional stop. Three typical expressions of the dislike of relief are illustrated by the personal histories of Herbert Randolph, Thomas Stribling, and Thad Carlton.

Herbert Randolph, a 37-year-old veteran, had been following migratory-casual work for 17 years. During the first part of this period he was employed largely in logging camps on the Pacific coast and in Idaho, but recently he has been doing work of all sorts— marine fireman, extra-gang laborer, apple picker, and oil-field worker.

He did not have a regular off-season although he said that when he was working in the logging camps he periodically took lay-offs of a week or so and then returned to the same job. Otherwise, his practice was to accumulate $100 and to travel until the money was gone.

The largest sum he had ever made during a single year was $1,200, earned in 1924. In 1932 he earned nothing; in 1933 as a seaman, logger, and section-hand he earned a total of $50; and in 1934, $100 on a logging job at Sand Point, Idaho.

Herbert Randolph had been to Washington, D. C., on the first bonus march, and said he had been "on the bum" for over a year after that. Early in 1934 he "just happened to see a cabin that could be lived in by fixing a couple of windows" in Whatcom County, Wash. He had repaired it and settled down for nearly a year.

He was jovial, but rather cynical. He complained of the poor food served him at the local shelter, and said he guessed he would have to find some kind of a job "because he just couldn't stand that stuff." He referred to transient relief as "the bread line", and, although he had no specific plans for the future, he was anxious to leave the transient shelter as soon as possible.

Thomas Stribling, 50 years old, a native Texan, became an agricultural migratory-casual worker in 1927. From 1906 until 1927 Mr. Stribling had worked as a painter, carpenter, and cement finisher. A period of unemployment forced him to seek aid at a mission in Forth Worth. The mission secured a job for him as a cotton picker, and he has been following agricultural work in Texas ever since.

In 1933, a typical year for Mr. Stribling, he worked in six different places, on five different crops: worked as a general farm laborer at Handley, Tex., during February; picked fruit at Pharr, Tex., for a month in the spring; cultivated onions at Haymondville, Tex., through most of the summer; picked cucumbers at Mathis, Tex., for 1 month; picked berries at Lindale, Tex., early in the fall; and from September until December picked cotton at Sebastian and Corpus Christi. He spent 1934 in much the same way, but despite the fact that he kept reasonably busy during both 1933 and 1934, his earnings were only $300 each year.

Thomas Stribling was excessively apologetic about being on relief. The onion harvest, which had brought him to Dallas, was late in 1935, and, having no funds, he had been forced for the first time since 1927 to ask for help. He seemed to pride himself on the fact that he had learned to live on such a small yearly income; he was even content, for example, to sleep outdoors most of the year.

Thad Carlton, a Negro, 29 years old, became a migratory-casual worker in 1932, when replacement of Negro workers by white workers closed the opportunities for his employment as porter and bellboy in Chicago. His last "permanent job" was as porter in a night club in Memphis. When he lost that job, he hitch-hiked to California, partly because of the attraction of the climate, but mainly in hope of finding hotel work there. He had several jobs as a bootblack and car washer around Los Angeles, and when someone told him of work in the lettuce fields, he went there and found a job cutting, packing, and loading lettuce.

Thad Carlton was working on a truck in the lettuce fields in Imperial Valley when the shed packers struck for higher wages. Since he was a Negro, he was not permitted to join the A. F. of L. shed-packers' union, and as a result he had continued to work on the truck with armed guards until the strike was over. After the strike, his employer had sold the crop to a San Diego contractor, who brought in his own laborers, displacing Mr. Carlton and the other workers who lived on the lettuce farm.

Thad Carlton was proud of his record of being self-supporting throughout the greater part of the depression and was extremely "anxious to get off relief."

He described some of the ways of getting work. "You always hang around a car rack after a rain because they have extra work washing cars then." He also watched the papers for announcements of conventions, and would follow them up and apply for work in the hotels where the conventions were to be held.

Political Attitudes.

The difficulty which migratory-casual workers had experienced in finding employment had various effects upon their thinking. Almost all of them had been in some measure discouraged by their experiences; but this feeling of discouragement was mitigated, in most cases, by a belief that the lack of employment was a temporary phenomenon connected with the depression, and that the lean years would pass. There were some, however, particularly among those prematurely superannuated, who felt that there was something basically wrong with the economic system, and that their troubles were merely symptoms of a widespread and grave ailment affecting all society.

Their conceptions of the nature of the ailment, and its cause and cure, were various. As may be observed in their personal histories, their diagnoses and suggested cures had little in common.

Arthur Hagen, a native Kansan, 44 years old, spent most of his life following the wheat harvest as a migratory-casual worker. Beginning in 1912, he harvested wheat each summer from Kansas to Canada, and occasionally worked between times on extra gangs and in logging camps. After the war he continued to follow the wheat, and filled in between seasons with general farm work near Sioux City, Iowa.

Arthur Hagen gave an account of the good wages and large labor demand in the wheat harvest before the war, when the shortage and inefficiency of farm machinery had to be made up in manpower. So great was the need for help that he often worked 40 days consecutively. His principal method of finding jobs was to ask the country storekeepers to tell where there was a shortage of workers. The extreme casualness of harvest employment is shown by the fact that although he returned each season to the same locality, and often threshed on a farm several years in succession, he seldom knew his employers' names.

As the farming country in Montana opened up, about 1915, he began going there because "men are scarcer and wages higher in a new country." After 1923 he no longer went into Canada, and by

1929 he said that harvest work was "no good at all because by then they had a combine for every quarter-section and didn't need many men." Nevertheless, he continued to make the trip into the Dakotas each summer, although he had secured no harvest work whatever since 1931. In 1933 and 1934 he had been almost altogether without work of any sort, and had secured only four jobs lasting an average of a week apiece during these 2 years.

Arthur Hagen freely expounded his plan for "running the country", which he had often wanted to write up, except that "his spelling bothered him too much." His plan, as he explained it, was to pay everyone over 40 years of age $200 a month, to be raised by a manufacturers' tax on the goods which would be sold when the recipients of the payments began to spend. Meantime, every relief client was to be fingerprinted and his record filed at a "National Bureau of Identification." Each relief client would then be issued a statement certifying that he was "homeless." Afterwards, whenever the client wanted relief again, he would present his certificate and his fingerprints and be granted assistance without delay.

Arthur Hagen felt that unless profound economic changes were made, his generation would probably never return to work. He was afraid, however, that there would be a war before those changes could be made.

Sylvanus Spenser, 43 years old, had been an agricultural migratory-casual worker around the Dakotas for several years after he was discharged from the Army. Subsequently he had secured a job as a moving-picture operator. When he lost that job in 1929, he jumped a freight and resumed following the harvest and odd construction jobs through the West and Southwest. In 1933 and 1934 he held nine different jobs: picking cotton near Buckeye, Ariz.; digging potatoes at Idaho Falls, Idaho; doing odd jobs in a hospital at Joplin, Mo.; picking strawberries at Fayetteville, Ark.; painting houses in Tulsa, Okla.; harvesting wheat in North Dakota; and picking wild blackberries and working at an orphanage in Joplin.

Sylvanus Spenser declared that he didn't know what was going to happen to the country; also, that "he'd hate to say what he thinks will happen to the country." He read a great deal in the newspapers and listened to speeches over the radio (he thought Father Coughlin and Huey Long were both "very fine men") but spent most of his time looking for work. His opinion that the condition of the country was hopeless had not destroyed his hope of finding "steady work some place", and when interviewed, he was en route to the Yakima Valley, Wash., to seek work in the fruit harvest.

John Hill had been a butcher for 14 years when the war began. After he returned from the war he was restless, and, finding that ex-service men were "getting the breaks" on construction jobs, he sold his butcher shop and became a migratory-casual worker. Since 1922 he has been employed almost continuously on construction jobs throughout the West—on hydroelectric developments at Skagit, Rock Island, and Renton, Wash.; on tunnel jobs at San Francisco and Malone, Calif., and at Cascade Tunnel, Wash. From 1931 to the middle of 1933 he was a machine driller at Boulder Dam, and in the last months of 1933 he worked on highway construction near Las Vegas. In 1934 he worked on road construction at Kingman, Ariz., and in the fall, worked for 3 months on an irrigation tunnel near Casper, Wyo. Late in 1934 he secured a short job on a tunnel at Fort Peck Dam, Mont.

John Hill never worked more than a few months on a construction job without taking time off to rest and "get the smoke out of his lungs." When working on Cascade Tunnel, "a very smoky job", he would work 2 months, then go to Seattle for a month's rest. While working in the Southwest, he habitually took time off periodically and went either to the jungles, where he slept in the open and "sunned himself" until he was rested, or else went to Las Vegas, where he frequently lost his money gambling before he had time to rest on his savings.

John Hill said that he had never "felt the depression" (when interviewed at a transient bureau he was en route to a construction job at Grand Coulee Dam, Wash.). Because of his strength and health, and his skill as a machine miner, combined with his wide acquaintance with contractors throughout the West, John Hill had never been out of work long. Despite these advantages, however, he had never made more than $1,200 net during any year. His best years were in 1929 and 1930 when wages were high and when, living near town, he could take rest periods easily without losing too much time from work.

John Hill said that he "wasn't worried about politics", and that like 19 out of 20 of his fellow-workers, he had no voting residence— "a person's vote doesn't count anyway", he said.

George Zimmerman, 37 years old, was 1 of 11 children of German immigrant parents. Since his first job as a cement worker, secured when he was 13 years old, he has held over 100 migratory-casual jobs. Most of them have been in the eastern Washington fruit harvest, in fruit and fish canneries, and in the grain harvest of the Big Bend country of eastern Washington.

At one time, spring-cultivation work had enabled him to maintain a fairly complete year-round work pattern, but in the last few years, he reported, cultivation jobs had become almost entirely mechanized. His seasons were now beginning in June, with apple thinning.

George Zimmerman had several times attempted to leave migratory-casual work. He had had occasional jobs in Seattle warehouses, had once taken a correspondence course in automobile repairing, and had subsequently worked at the trade in Seattle for a short period. At another time, he had for 3 months sold automobiles. But his lack of education and his German accent always handicapped him, and because his early training made farm jobs the easiest to find and the best paid he could get, he had eventually confined himself entirely to them. His highest earning years were in the early 1920's. Since 1930 he had never made more than $300 a year and had earned only $125 in 1934.

George Zimmerman expressed fear that the depression would lead to war. When questioned further as to his attitudes, he wrote this reply:

Not being a writer, and being more used to watching and studying, I may not convey my ideas as I see them. But I will do my best to that end.

In order to be able to give work to more persons we must know as much as possible about the cause of unemployment. Industrialism claims the regaining of foreign markets will end the depression and unemployment. But they do not tell us that foreign countries are trying to do the same thing, trying to produce all their own needs and restore prosperity by exporting *their* surplus. So no help there.

Some of our unemployment is only for a time, caused by temporary depression. But most of those unemployed will never find work again yet. The reason for this is machines, which have taken the place of men in every branch of industry and farming. Much of the labor they displace is not again absorbed because employers do not increase the wages of the men they keep enough to stimulate them to buy products of other industries, or lower prices enough to increase demand to where production increases will reemploy laid-off men.

But let us not blame the machine—to do away with it would be to increase production cost, prices, which would decrease consumption and cause more unemployment. It is the system which is at fault.

Put more profit in the hands of the employees, so they can buy back that which is produced by their labor. Greedy employers will not do this, so government must; government of the people, by the people, for the people. All people have the right to a chance to earn a decent living and our government must prevent any minority from causing depression by uncontrolled use of money and profit.

I do not say divide the wealth. But we should make a reasonable limit to a person's wealth. I believe in government ownership of all natural resources and public serving institutions. I come to this conclusion through more than 20 years of work, study, and observation all over the United States.

CHAPTER VI

CONCLUSIONS

THE EVIDENCE OF this report points clearly to the conclusion that the migratory-casual worker, despite his independent attitude and his pride in his ability to "get by" on the road, is in fact an underemployed and poorly paid worker, who easily and frequently becomes a charge on society. Directly or indirectly, State and local governments are forced to accept some responsibility for individuals in this group. Hospitalization, emergency relief, border patrols, and the policing of jungles, shantytowns, and scenes of labor disputes are examples of money costs that are borne directly by the public. Moreover, it must be remembered that many of the local homeless of the large cities who are dependent on public or private assistance—those who fill the municipal lodging houses, missions, and cheap flop houses at night, or sleep on park benches, docks, and in subways—are discards from the ranks of the migratory-casual worker, since by reason of age, habits, or infirmities, they are no longer able to make a living on the road.

There is another cost that cannot be assessed in dollars: the existence of a group whose low earnings necessitate a standard of living far below the level of decency and comfort. The presence of such a group in any community, even though for a short time each year, cannot fail to affect adversely the wage level of resident workers who are engaged in the same or similar pursuits.

The social and economic problem growing out of inadequate employment at low wages is, of course, not confined to the migratory-casual worker. Millions of resident workers have been, or are now, dependent upon unemployment relief because of these same inadequacies. The problem of the migratory-casual worker is one aspect of the general problem of economic insecurity, but, because of the economic function involved, its relation to the larger problem is peculiar.

The migratory-casual worker exists because of the labor demand of agricultural and industrial processes that operate seasonally or intermittently in areas where the resident population does not supply the necessary labor force. The demand arises from operations associated with the progression of the seasons; and the supply comes from among the more mobile individuals that compose the general pool of unemployed.

This integral relationship of the migratory-casual worker to the total labor supply is sometimes overlooked. The thinking that has from time to time been given to a solution of the problem presented has overemphasized the unique character of migratory-casual employment. Solutions commonly suggested are: (1) assisting the worker to establish employment sequences through dovetailing employment in processes differing as to time of peak operations; and (2) stabilizing the migrant worker through off-season employment in related or nonrelated operations.

These proposals are not entirely consistent, since the line of thought in (1) is based upon the assumption that a mobile labor force is essential to these processes, while in (2) this assumption is denied. Public employment offices would provide the mechanism for facilitating employment sequences, while it is primarily the employer, perhaps aided by employment offices, who would arrange the off-season employment necessary for stabilization.

There is sufficient evidence in this report to permit a critical examination of both these proposals. Any plan to develop employment sequences extending over a major part of the year runs counter to the fact shown in chapter IV that both agricultural and industrial processes employing mobile labor reach their peaks of labor demand at about the same period of the year—late spring to early fall—and that for a good number, the peaks of employment coincide. Under these circumstances, employment sequences exceeding one-half of the year are impossible for all the workers employed during the summer months.. This conclusion does not overlook the fact that some workers follow logging in the winter and harvesting in the summer, or that some extra-gang workers fill in the winter as general farm hands. These and similar sequences occur, but by the very nature of the unequal labor demand of the summer, as against that of the winter months, all, or even a substantial proportion, of the mobile reserve cannot secure such sequences of employment.

Another objection must be raised against dependence upon public employment offices to spread employment among migrants. During periods of depression, when the general pool of unemployment rises by reason of wholesale layoffs of resident workers, the effectiveness of employment offices in directing the movement of the migratory-casual worker would be seriously restricted. When there is a general surplus of workers, employment offices, like business establishments, have little market for their offerings. The experience of the past few years shows that resident workmen turn migrants in sufficient numbers to provide serious competition to the habitual migratory-casual worker in those seasonal operations—particularly in agriculture—that continue in good times and in bad. During such times what is needed is not employment office direction of the labor reserve, swollen with newcomers, into areas where it will compete for the jobs ordinarily held by habitual migratory-casual workers. Instead, what is needed is the diversion of the surplus into such channels as public works, for the purpose of lessening the progressive disorganization of the labor market.

Although it is a conclusion of this study that the direction of the migratory-casual worker by employment offices would not provide a basic solution of the problem, plainly such direction could assist materially in reducing the intensity of the problem. By anticipating local demands for seasonal labor, and exchanging this information with other offices in the same area, they could do much to restrict the extent of migration illustrated in chapter II of this report. Furthermore, if these offices could become the means of impounding the surplus of mobile workmen through diversion to public works projects during depressions, migratory and resident workmen alike would benefit. Any such procedure would, of course, run counter to the deeply rooted custom that "residents come first" which is to be found in the settlement laws on the statute books of most of the States.

The second of the proposals mentioned above—stabilization of the migratory-casual worker—needs but scant attention here. It is obviously unworkable except in such industrial operations as lumbering, where the seasonality of employment is largely the result of market conditions that conceivably could be controlled. Mention was made in chapter I of the efforts of a large sugar-beet company to find off-season employment for its migratory workers. Because of the relatively long employment season in sugar beets it would seem to provide an exceptionally favorable opportunity for attempting stabilization. But here, as elsewhere, stabilization would depend on some seasonal operation—existing or to be devised—that complements the principal employment season. The difficulty of finding existing off-season operations seems to be self-evident; and operations devised to use this off-season excess of labor have generally led to even more than ordinary exploitation.[1]

No doubt something could be done toward stabilization of agricultural workers in some States, such as California, which have an almost continuous growing season. Some relative degree of stabilization might be achieved through the staggering of the planting. However, two careful students of agricultural labor point out that:

> Reorganization of crop plantings in order to regularize demand for farm labor, and so to stabilize it, has long been urged in California. But considerations of market, soil, and climate, rather than conservation

---

[1] As an example of how operations planned to use migratory workers during the off-season, see the testimony concerning the Grays Harbor Commercial Co., in the Report of the Commission on Industrial Relations, S. Doc. No. 415, 64th Cong., Washington, D. C., 1916, vol. V, p. 4285 ff.

of labor power and the human resources of the laborer, continue to govern. On the whole they impede stabilization.[2]

No mention has been made up to this point of the possible effect of the unemployment insurance provision of the Social Security Act on the problem of the migratory-casual worker. In its present form unemployment insurance can be of little or no direct benefit to this group. In the first place, agriculture, the largest employer of migratory-casual workers, is an "uncovered industry." In the second place, migratory-casual workers in the covered industries are either specifically excluded from benefits (e. g., in Massachusetts) or, what in most cases amounts to the same thing, will be excluded because of failure to meet the requirement of a minimum period of employment in covered industries within the State [3] (see ch. III on duration of jobs). Even workers having employment in covered industries in excess of the minimum requirement may be excluded because this employment was held in two or more States.[4]

Assuming, as seems reasonable, that coverage will be broadened, there arises the nice problem of how the migratory-casual worker, with his preponderantly short-term jobs and frequent movement across State lines, would be handled administratively under an insurance plan. Moreover, the yearly earnings of migratory-casual workers in both agriculture and industry are so small (see ch. III) that benefits would be of little help even if the other difficulties could be surmounted.

Indirectly, however, unemployment insurance should work to the benefit of the migratory-casual worker. It has been pointed out repeatedly in this report that the general instability of industrial employment creates a pool of unemployed from which come many of the migratory-casual workers. Insofar as unemployment insurance for resident workmen reduces this source of pressure on the labor market it will assist the migratory-casual worker, particularly during depressions. Moreover, the unemployment-insurance laws of many States, by rewarding the reduction of labor turnover, may tend toward

---

[2] Taylor, Paul S., and Vasey, Tom, Contemporary Background of California Farm Labor, Rural Sociology, December 1936, pp. 416–417.

[3] At the time this report was written, 36 States had unemployment compensation laws in effect. All of them contained a provision for a minimum period of employment in covered industries within the State during the preceding 52 weeks. The most liberal provision was 13 weeks, and the least liberal, 26 weeks.

[4] See Burns, Eveline M., Towards Social Security, Whittlesey House, New York, 1936, pp. 84–85.

"Migratory workers will have difficulty in obtaining benefits even if they work for a time in States with compensation laws * * *. Even a worker who has had jobs in two States, both providing unemployment compensation, may lose his rights. His period of work in each State may be too short to permit him to claim benefits, although when added together they would amount to the minimum period required by the laws of either State."

stabilization of both employment and workers;[5] and it may well be that the covered industrial processes thus affected may, in becoming less seasonal and intermittent, reduce the necessity for the migration of workers.

Because of its essentially seasonal nature, agricultural employment presents the major problem that must be solved if the migratory-casual worker is to improve his status. The prospects here are not encouraging, although it should be noted that in many sections of the country the increase of population density has brought with it a solution of a kind. For instance, the New Jersey truck farms are as dependent upon seasonal labor as are those of the Imperial Valley in California. But New Jersey farmers can draw upon the local unemployed of Philadelphia, Camden, and other lesser urban centers for workers that more nearly resemble underpaid commuters than they do the agricultural migratory workers of the West.[6]

Thus, the population pattern may, in its development, reduce or remove the need for the habitual migrant. Certainly the function of the migratory-casual worker decreases in importance or disappears when a surplus of labor is available locally. It will be recalled that few of the 500 migratory-casual workers in this study made excursions into the Old South, where the supply of Negro workers is adequate to handle all seasonal work.

In summary, there does not appear to be any immediate solution of the social and economic problem presented by the habitual migratory-casual worker. The most promising means of reducing the intensity of the problem appears to lie in some degree of employment-office control involving a high degree of cooperation among offices, employers, and workers; and, during depression periods, the diversion of the surplus to public works. However, the possibility of the workers themselves improving conditions through unionization cannot be ignored. It is true that organization is extraordinarily difficult because of the high mobility and the low earnings of these workers; but the recent success of union campaigns

---

[5] I. e., through the operation of the merit-rating clauses, the individual-plant-reserve plans, and guaranteed employment.

"Opinions differ greatly as to how far unemployment will be reduced by these methods. The most serious kinds of unemployment are, after all, outside the control of any individual employer * * *. At most he can control minor fluctuations. Some ways of stabilizing production may be quite costly and may even counterbalance any gain through a reduction in his payroll tax." See Burns, Eveline M., op. cit., p. 74.

[6] This use of urban laborers is already under way in California, according to Taylor and Vasey (op. cit., p. 408):

"The tenuousness of the connection of California farm laborers with the farm is further emphasized by their residence. While 74.4 percent of paid farm laborers in Mississippi and 77.4 percent in Iowa resided on the farm in 1930, only 43.5 percent resided ,on the farm in California. In Mississippi 5.2 percent, and in Iowa 7.6 percent of paid farm laborers had urban residence. But in California 28.6 percent were urban."

among the loggers in the Pacific Northwest and in Minnesota, the seamen on both coasts, and the fruit and vegetable workers of California shows that organization of migratory-casual workers is far from impossible.

Aside from the means summarized above there does not, on the basis of this study, appear to be any other possibility of full or partial solution—except for the contingency of unforeseen economic developments—short of those eventual and unhurried changes in population patterns that promise to eliminate the economic function of the migratory-casual worker. This solution can be fully approved only by those who oppose any attempt to alter the working of the "natural laws" of our economy.

APPENDIX

APPENDIX

TABLE 1.—NUMBER OF MIGRATORY-CASUAL WORKERS IN 13 STUDY-CITIES

City	All workers	Type of worker		
		Agricultural	Industrial	Combination [1]
Total	500	200	100	200
Boston, Mass	17			17
Chicago, Ill	12	1	5	6
Dallas, Tex	30	11	12	7
Denver, Colo	79	18	20	41
Jacksonville, Fla	24	4		20
Kansas City, Mo	21	5	6	10
Los Angeles, Calif	56	35	11	10
Memphis, Tenn	62	25	13	24
Minneapolis, Minn	61	33	16	12
New Orleans, La	20	15		5
Phoenix, Ariz	24	17		7
Pittsburgh, Pa	4			4
Seattle, Wash	90	36	17	37

[1] Workers combining agricultural and industrial employment.

TABLE 2.—STATE OF PRINCIPAL EMPLOYMENT [1] OF 500 MIGRATORY-CASUAL WORKERS, 1933–34

State of principal employment [1]	1933				1934			
	All workers	Type of worker			All workers	Type of worker		
		Agricultural	Industrial	Combination [2]		Agricultural	Industrial	Combination [2]
Total	500	200	100	200	500	200	100	200
Alabama	4		2	2	3		1	2
Arizona	7	6		1	13	10	1	2
Arkansas	30	13	5	12	29	11	4	14
California	48	27	8	13	51	29	9	13
Colorado	19	10	1	8	20	10	2	8
Connecticut	1			1				
Florida	10	4		6	11	3	1	7
Georgia	5	1		4	4	1		3
Idaho	6	3		3	5	2		3
Illinois	4		2	2	2		2	
Indiana	4		1	3	2		1	1
Iowa	4	3		1	8	2	4	2
Kansas	16	7		9	14	2	3	9
Kentucky	2	1		1	4	2	1	1
Louisiana	10	3	5	2	10	4	3	3
Maine	6		2	4	6		2	4
Maryland	1			1				
Massachusetts	3			3	4	1		3
Michigan	11	7	1	3	10	6	1	3
Minnesota	42	26	8	8	41	27	8	6

111

TABLE 2.—STATE OF PRINCIPAL EMPLOYMENT OF 500 MIGRATORY-CASUAL WORKERS, 1933–34—Continued

State of principal employment	1933				1934			
	All workers	Type of worker			All workers	Type of worker		
		Agricultural	Industrial	Combination		Agricultural	Industrial	Combination
Mississippi	6		2	4	6	1	2	3
Missouri	22	5	9	8	16	4	5	7
Montana	10	4	2	4	14	6	2	6
Nebraska	13	6	1	6	16	5	3	8
Nevada	4	1	2	1	5		3	2
New Hampshire	1			1	1			1
New Mexico	5		2	3	10	2	2	6
New Jersey	1		1		1		1	
New York	11	2	2	7	6	1		5
North Carolina	1			1	1			1
North Dakota	15	9	1	5	10	5		5
Ohio	4		1	3	4		2	2
Oklahoma	16	8	4	4	17	8	3	6
Oregon	10	3	2	5	10	4	2	4
Pennsylvania	8		2	6	3		1	2
South Dakota	2	1	1					
Tennessee	5		1	4	5		1	4
Texas	32	15	9	8	31	14	7	10
Utah	1		1		1		1	
Washington	49	23	12	14	53	24	12	17
West Virginia	1			1				
Wisconsin	9	1	5	3	9	2	4	3
Wyoming	11	3		8	15	5	3	7
Alaska	1		1		1			1
Not ascertainable	7		1	6	6		1	5
No State [3]	22	8	3	11	22	9	2	11

[1] Maximum employment in a State.
[2] Workers combining agricultural and industrial employment.
[3] I. e., workers unemployed.

TABLE 3.—MONTH OF OBTAINING JOBS, 500 MIGRATORY-CASUAL WORKERS, 1933–34

Month	1933				1934			
	All jobs	Jobs of agricultural workers	Jobs of industrial workers	Jobs of combination workers[1]	All jobs	Jobs of agricultural workers	Jobs of industrial workers	Jobs of combination workers[1]
Total	1,190	486	228	476	[2] 1,107	[3] 471	[4] 205	[5] 431
January	[6] 131	[6] 38	[6] 33	[6] 60	83	23	12	48
February	44	14	12	18	53	21	13	19
March	78	26	12	40	62	20	15	27
April	90	36	23	31	81	37	14	30
May	117	54	27	36	115	55	30	30
June	118	51	25	42	124	57	26	41
July	123	57	20	46	126	55	19	52
August	102	46	17	39	107	50	15	42
September	145	76	24	45	133	70	23	40
October	98	49	12	37	91	42	11	38
November	75	24	12	39	39	7	10	22
December	43	7	9	27	23	7	7	9
Not ascertainable	26	8	2	16	6		1	5

[1] Jobs of workers combining agricultural and industrial employment.
[2] Includes 64 jobs which were continuations of jobs obtained in 1933.
[3] Includes 27 jobs which were continuations of jobs obtained in 1933.
[4] Includes 9 jobs which were continuations of jobs obtained in 1933.
[5] Includes 28 jobs which were continuations of jobs obtained in 1933.
[6] An unknown number of January jobs were continuations of jobs obtained in 1932.

TABLE 4.—DURATION OF OFF-SEASON OF 500 MIGRATORY-CASUAL WORKERS, 1933–34

Duration of off-season	1933				1934			
	Total	Type of worker			Total	Type of worker		
		Agricultural	Industrial	Combination [1]		Agricultural	Industrial	Combination [1]
All workers	500	200	100	200	500	200	100	200
	Percent distribution							
All workers	100	100	100	100	100	100	100	100
Less than 4 weeks	41	35	45	46	42	35	44	49
4 to 11 weeks	8	8	9	8	7	7	9	6
12 to 19 weeks	30	33	22	26	30	34	32	25
20 to 27 weeks	15	16	13	14	15	17	15	14
28 to 51 weeks	3	5	1	1	2	4		1
52 weeks	3	3		5	4	3		5
Median duration of off-season in weeks	11	13	7	7	11	13	8	4

[1] Workers combining agricultural and industrial employment.

TABLE 5.—TIME SPENT IN EMPLOYMENT DURING MIGRATORY PERIOD BY 500 MIGRATORY-CASUAL WORKERS, 1933–34

Time spent in employment	Type of worker							
	Total		Agricultural		Industrial		Combination [1]	
	1933	1934	1933	1934	1933	1934	1933	1934
All workers	500	500	200	200	100	100	200	200
	Percent distribution							
All workers	100	100	100	100	100	100	100	100
No employment	5	5	4	5	3	3	5	5
Less than 10 weeks	14	19	13	18	8	15	18	23
10 to 20 weeks	24	26	27	24	28	21	20	31
21 to 32 weeks	29	32	29	36	27	43	31	23
33 to 40 weeks	14	11	14	10	15	10	14	12
40 to 52 weeks	12	7	12	7	17	8	10	6
Not ascertainable	2		1		2		2	
Median time spent in employment, in weeks	24	21	23	22	26	24	23	18

[1] Workers combining agricultural and industrial employment.

TABLE 6.—NET YEARLY EARNINGS OF 500 MIGRATORY-CASUAL WORKERS, 1933–34

| Amount of earnings | 1933 | | | | 1934 | | | |
| | All workers | Type of worker | | | All workers | Type of worker | | |
		Agricultural	Industrial	Combination [1]		Agricultural	Industrial	Combination [1]
Total	500	200	100	200	500	200	100	200
None	18	6	1	11	21	9	1	11
Maintenance only	2	1	1		2		2	
$0 to $49	47	24	6	17	49	30	5	14
$50 to $99	79	55	6	18	74	37	12	25
$100 to $149	69	41	8	20	69	39	7	23
$150 to $199	61	24	16	21	63	27	13	23
$200 to $249	48	18	9	21	48	19	5	24
$250 to $299	34	8	14	12	46	14	10	22
$300 to $349	33	5	10	18	21	4	8	9
$350 to $399	18	2	6	10	23	4	7	12
$400 to $499	24	1	5	18	27	2	12	13
$500 to $599	20	3	8	9	14	2	7	5
$600 to $699	6		1	5	9		3	6
$700 to $999	14		5	9	11	1	5	5
$1,000 to $1,350	4		1	3	3		1	2
Not ascertainable	23	12	3	8	20	12	2	6

[1] Workers combining agricultural and industrial employment.

TABLE 7.—MAN-WEEKS OF EMPLOYMENT AND NUMBER OF JOBS OF 500 MIGRATORY-CASUAL WORKERS, CLASSIFIED BY TYPE OF WORKER AND BY SPECIFIC CROPS AND PROCESSES, 1933–34

| Type of worker and pursuit | Number of jobs | | | Man-weeks of employment | | |
	Total	1933	1934	Total	1933	1934
All workers	2,297	1,190	1,107	21,128.5	11,182.0	9,946.5
Agricultural workers:						
All agricultural workers	957	486	471	8,171.5	4,264.5	3,907.0
Cotton	156	87	69	1,401.5	790.0	611.5
Fruits	193	97	96	1,318.0	697.0	621.0
Sugar beets	86	40	46	1,253.0	608.0	645.0
Grain	154	77	77	1,121.5	603.0	518.5
General agriculture	69	32	37	935.0	443.0	492.0
Vegetables	94	48	46	687.0	362.0	325.0
Berries	97	46	51	611.0	300.0	311.0
Dairy and cattle	32	17	15	418.0	195.0	223.0
Other, n. e. c.[1]	76	42	34	426.5	266.5	160.0
Industrial workers:						
All industrial workers	433	228	205	4,767.5	2,522.5	2,245.0
Logging	68	36	32	906.0	476.0	430.0
Oil and gas	59	31	28	585.0	297.0	288.0
Agriculture	64	31	33	549.0	244.0	305.0
Railroad maintenance	46	21	25	516.0	229.0	287.0
Road construction	34	21	13	445.0	295.0	150.0
Dam and levee	30	16	14	424.5	217.5	207.0
Seamen	41	23	18	406.0	240.0	166.0
Other construction [2]	22	12	10	206.0	116.0	90.0
Metals (mining)	23	11	12	203.0	100.0	103.0
Other, n. e. c.[1]	46	26	20	527.0	308.0	219.0

TABLE 7.—MAN-WEEKS OF EMPLOYMENT AND NUMBER OF JOBS OF 500 MIGRATORY-CASUAL WORKERS, CLASSIFIED BY TYPE OF WORKER AND BY SPECIFIC CROPS AND PROCESSES, 1933–34—Continued

Type of worker and pursuit	Number of jobs			Man-weeks of employment		
	Total	1933	1934	Total	1933	1934
Combination workers: [3]						
All combination workers	907	476	431	8,189.5	4,395.0	3,794.5
General agriculture	56	31	25	910.0	465.0	445.0
Road construction	79	46	33	842.0	486.0	356.0
Logging	78	40	38	800.5	416.0	384.5
Seamen	95	52	43	778.0	460.0	318.0
Grain	88	49	39	660.5	409.0	251.5
Cotton	61	34	27	465.0	280.0	185.0
Dam and levee	27	15	12	430.0	233.0	197.0
Railroad maintenance	48	16	32	385.0	130.0	255.0
Dairy and cattle	34	18	16	385.0	218.0	167.0
Building construction	42	20	22	357.5	146.0	211.5
Fruits	57	31	26	348.0	195.5	152.5
Sawmilling	25	17	8	237.0	141.0	96.0
Sugar beets	28	17	11	181.0	106.0	75.0
Other agricultural, n. e. c.[1]	99	45	54	508.5	224.5	284.0
Other industrial, n. e. c.[1]	90	45	45	901.5	485.0	416.5

[1] Not elsewhere classified.
[2] "Other construction" represents workers in tunnel, bridge, and building construction.
[3] Workers combining agricultural and industrial employments.

TABLE 8.—SEASONAL FLUCTUATION IN EMPLOYMENT IN ALL PURSUITS AND IN SELECTED PURSUITS, 200 AGRICULTURAL WORKERS, 1933–34

Month and year	All pursuits	Man-weeks of employment								
		Selected pursuits								
		Cotton	Fruits	Sugar beets	Grain	General agriculture	Vegetables	Berries	Dairy and cattle	Hops
1933										
January	162	41	26	4	9	30	26	13	9	
February	184	40	39	4	7	30	29	17	9	
March	208	39	35	9	4	37	13	58	4	
April	263	49	39	15	12	52	20	50	9	
May	397	55	60	100	22	65	23	49	13	
June	460	46	86	104	68	56	26	38	17	
July	519	52	110	102	100	30	31	35	26	4
August	527	56	95	88	142	39	24	17	28	9
September	555	110	76	98	96	32	55	11	17	34
October	461	127	68	68	74	24	41	9	17	4
November	328	118	37	12	48	26	41	2	22	
December	186	58	21	4	20	18	32		24	
1934										
January	216	48	35	4	11	52	35		22	
February	240	36	35		13	58	56	4	28	
March	270	43	27	9	17	75	37	30	26	
April	304	47	46	13	21	80	11	42	38	
May	420	35	49	111	29	71	18	73	30	
June	439	30	49	108	89	52	14	67	22	
July	481	43	78	100	109	32	17	59	22	
August	459	53	103	104	91	25	30	19	9	6
September	465	88	97	101	57	16	35	11	11	36
October	358	101	53	74	45	11	38	4	13	11
November	189	65	32	21	26	9	28	2	2	
December	64	22	16		9	11	6			

TABLE 9.—SEASONAL FLUCTUATION IN EMPLOYMENT IN ALL PURSUITS AND IN SELECTED PURSUITS, 100 INDUSTRIAL WORKERS, 1933–34

Month and year	All pursuits	Man-weeks of employment							
		Selected pursuits							
		Logging	Oil and gas	Agriculture	Railroad maintenance	Dam and levee construction	Seamen	Road construction	Other construction
1933									
January	136	52	22		4	4	10	17	4
February	169	52	29		9	4	11	17	4
March	171	56	27	7	9	4	9	22	4
April	216	48	31	14	17	9	15	26	13
May	232	35	33	28	30	17	14	25	17
June	281	35	35	39	35	26	23	34	16
July	284	35	30	33	37	30	26	35	15
August	270	22	23	38	39	22	28	39	15
September	278	30	29	47	29	26	30	35	18
October	192	35	12	21	18	22	28	26	4
November	175	37	15	13	2	30	33	10	4
December	118	39	11	4		23	13	9	2
1934									
January	92	39	9	4		4	9	4	8
February	122	48	13	7	13	11	13	1	8
March	165	61	17	9	22	9	13	4	13
April	165	50	13	15	13	27	9	9	12
May	223	35	35	26	37	22	23	15	10
June	275	30	54	36	48	19	22	30	8
July	281	26	46	54	56	26	15	24	4
August	242	22	22	41	45	30	20	22	10
September	244	28	31	39	34	24	13	24	7
October	200	35	22	40	10	22	13	9	4
November	149	30	17	26	4	13	7	4	4
December	86	26	9	8	4		9	4	2

TABLE 10.—SEASONAL FLUCTUATION IN EMPLOYMENT IN ALL PURSUITS AND IN SELECTED PURSUITS, 200 COMBINATION WORKERS,[1] 1933–34

Month and year	All pursuits	Man-weeks of employment							
		Selected pursuits							
		General agriculture	Road construction	Logging	Grain	Cotton	Dam and levee construction	Railroad maintenance	Dairy and cattle
1933									
January	241	35	23	39	4	13		4	17
February	275	39	52	43	4	6		12	17
March	366	43	67	26	9	13	17	9	22
April	361	65	61	26	4	13	22	13	26
May	425	54	52	28	17	24	22	17	19
June	454	48	48	26	61	22	28	17	16
July	439	37	40	19	99	29	30	23	17
August	434	36	51	35	103	17	37	13	15
September	388	39	27	36	56	54	28		13
October	378	35	17	32	32	61	26	4	17
November	307	17	22	53	13	18	19	11	17
December	239	17	22	49	7	10	4	7	22
1934									
January	306	30	39	45	9	0	13	12	30
February	298	35	45	39	4	4	9	4	24
March	362	52	50	43	9	13	22	4	26
April	352	65	39	24	13	17	13	30	22
May	357	56	26	22	13	22	22	28	17
June	372	56	37	26	31	15	30	20	18
July	411	43	28	28	43	14	30	37	13
August	403	35	35	24	45	17	19	36	13
September	332	27	24	26	34	39	17	29	4
October	290	27	22	37	26	28	13	31	
November	183	15	5	40	16	6	9	18	
December	83	4	6	26	8	9		6	

[1] Workers combining agricultural and industrial employment.

INDEX

INDEX